ADVANCE PRAISE FOR ... STOMER SERVICE

Lisa Ford, David McNair, and Bill Perry have achieved something truly rare indeed: a business book providing clear instructions for delivering world class customer service that is an absolute joy to read. In a world where high quality is now the rule rather than the exception, it is the quality of the service that differentiates a company from its competition. The "whys" and "hows" are all here, and after reading this book one is left with this certainty: "Yes. I can do this!"

Just imagine . . . increase profits, build and maintain profitable relationships with fiercely loyal customers, and have fun in the process. Does it get any better than that?

—Gary W. Henderson
Manager, Special Consumer Services,
Ben & Jerry's Homemade, Inc.

* * *

Anyone seeking service excellence, including managers who design service policies and the employees who put those policies into practice, will find this book excellent reading. Lisa Ford, David McNair, and Bill Perry offer practical, logical information that inspires both creativity and innovation in the service marketplace.

—John Bachmann
Managing Partner
Edward Jones

* * *

After reading this book, you will want to be a "Service Star" for the rest of your life. The authors provide a set of useful tools which will assist every individual in an organization to proactively achieve the type of consistent, exceptional service all customers deserve.

—Barbe West, Regional President
Kaiser Permanente

* * *

Exceptional Customer Service elevates customer service from an over-used, generic phrase to its rightful position as the key ingredient for success. Ford, McNair, and Perry show that whether you're a frontline service provider or a manager behind the scenes, in a company big or small, you've got to be open to change. Through examples, anecdotes, and exercises, this book helps you reevaluate every part of your business and teaches you how to treat customers with the right amount of accessibility and care.

—Steve Morris
Fortune 500 Executive

* * *

In *Exceptional Customer Service*, Ford, McNair, and Perry have put their fingers on the true keys to customer service excellence in a globally competitive marketplace.

—William A. Finn
Chairman and CEO
AstenJohnson, Inc.

EXCEPTIONAL CUSTOMER SERVICE

★★★ ★★★

EXCEPTIONAL CUSTOMER SERVICE

Going Beyond Your Good Service to Exceed the Customer's Expectation

Lisa Ford
David McNair
Bill Perry

Adams Media Corporation
Avon, Massachusetts

Published by
Adams Media, an F+W Publications Company
57 Littlefield Street, Avon, MA 02322. U.S.A.
www.adamsmedia.com

ISBN 13: 978-1-58062-458-9
ISBN 10: 1-58062-458-8

Printed in Canada.

J I H

Library of Congress Cataloging-in-Publication
information available from the publisher.

This publication is designed to provide accurate and authoritative information with regard
to the subject matter covered. It is sold with the understanding that the publisher is not
engaged in rendering legal, accounting, or other professional advice. If legal advice or other
expert assistance is required, the services of a competent professional person should be
sought.

—From a *Declaration of Principles* jointly adopted by a
Committee of the American Bar Association and
a Committee of Publishers and Associations

"Bullseye" cartoons copyright ©McNair/Nation.

This book is available at quantity discounts for bulk purchases.
For information, call 1-800-289-0963.

Contents

Foreword

How better to introduce you to this book than to tell you just why I like it. There's been much written about customer service through the years. Just look in the bookstores and Internet libraries, and see the vast materials available on customer service. That's not surprising when you consider that we, in the service profession, have been at this business of trying to please—better yet, to delight—customers since the beginning of time.

Consider the phrase "customer service." We gloss over it in speaking and we print it on signs, in brochures, and in advertisements. How often do we stop and think of the profound implications of those two simple words? As for customer, each of us walks in these shoes every day. You would think that alone makes us eminently qualified to evaluate, critique, and, hopefully, improve our own service delivery. Also, as customers we are better educated, have vastly greater access to information, and, most of all, have far more choices for buying goods and services than did our parents.

All of which makes the second word, service, such a very important part of the phrase. All the research shows that today's consumer makes buying decisions based 10 percent on product and 90 percent on service. But, if you do not receive the service, the value of the product, then you did not get what you paid for. Enough said?

I am no stranger to customer service. Ritz-Carlton Hotels are often cited as one of the world's true icons of exceptional customer service. Of this, I am personally very proud. For our people, who serve so willingly and tirelessly, I am truly and deeply grateful. A question that I am asked repeatedly, "How do you instill such a consistently high level of service?" I wish I had a simple answer for. My short answer is our people. Our people truly and genuinely care. We believe in "moving heaven and earth" to make our guests happy but also realize that two ingredients are necessary for that to occur: culture (philosophy) and a plan. The service culture must start at the top and, through shared vision and values, permeate the entire organization. Exceptional service comes from our people and your people. At the same time it must be backed by a strong service culture, training, technology, and systems that empower us to serve. It centers on our Credo, our 20 Basics, and again, our people.

Exceptional Customer Service speaks to frontline associates, managers/leaders, CEOs, and owners alike. It's not hype; it's real issues with real solutions . . . not to mention some great humor mixed in. It's a text that brings you the practical do's and don'ts that have made Lisa Ford's videos the best-selling training series in the United States. Whether you are a tire dealer in South Carolina, a dry cleaner in California, or a major manufacturer in the Northeast, this book can and will help you. It talks retail, it talks professional service firms, it talks business-to-business and most everything in between. *Exceptional Customer Service* has tips, team and individual exercises, humorous cartoons, and most of all, real-life anecdotes from the authors to bring home the experiences of poor and exceptional service.

I join these authors in encouraging you to make a difference in how we serve. Begin your journey to exceptional customer service today and set the standards for others to follow. You'll be glad you did!

Horst H. Schulze
President, Chief Operating Officer
Ritz-Carlton Hotels

Preface

If there is a common denominator shared by all organizations—public or private, large or small, manufacturing, service, or government—it is the critical need for exceptional customer service. Unfortunately, the uncommon denominator today seems to be the organization that truly believes in and practices exceptional customer care. This is why we have written this book. It's a how to; it has steps, tips, and exercises. It's an individual and/or team guidebook that provides a roadmap for changing service attitudes and behaviors.

It is difficult to think of a business (including e-business), industry, government, nonprofit, or other type organization that doesn't live or die by its customer focus. Even the much-maligned Internal Revenue Service is being forced through public and congressional pressure to become more customer friendly. Because the quality of customer service is continuously evaluated by consumers in day-to-day business interactions, the phrase from Shakespeare's *As You Like It*, "All the world's a stage, and all the men and women merely players," accurately describes the role of service providers.

Given the importance of customer care, it should be no surprise that more than 600 books currently exist on the subject. Many are excellent; some generate enthusiasm and resolve that propel one to the office the next day to revolutionize customer service. Most of these books fall short, however, in one major respect. Providing exceptional customer service requires behavior modification on the part of executives, managers, and frontline workers alike. Modifying behavior requires persistence, perspiration, and most of all, practice. An amateur golfer can go to Augusta, watch the Masters Tournament, and become inspired to upgrade his game to the professional level. To actually improve, however, requires reading books, watching tapes, taking lessons, and practicing endlessly. In the same way, *Southern Living* and *Architectural Digest* can provide countless ideas on redecorating a house; the actual work requires a how-to book.

Exceptional Customer Service: Going Beyond Your Good Service to Exceed the Customer's Expectation is the book organizations need today. It is based on a combined 70 years of knowledge and practical experience of the authors. What has previously been shared on video and in seminars with millions of people around the world is now in print to be taken home or to the office with practical methods of improving customer service.

We expect readers of *Exceptional Customer Service* to underline, highlight, and dog-ear the pages. We've included numerous exercises that are designed to assess current customer service levels and then eliminate the gap between current and world-class service. We encourage you to make copies of these exercises and use them in team meetings.

It is our hope that you will find *Exceptional Customer Service* a fun book to read. Cartoons by widely published illustrator Tate Nation bring examples to light in a humorous yet educational manner. Real-life anecdotes have been sprinkled liberally throughout the manuscript. Most of all, *Exceptional Customer Service* is a well-researched, interactive, highly practical guide for creating a true customer experience.

In writing this book, we have taken into consideration the current trend toward flatter business structures and the use of teams. We have also included the technological impacts of today, including the evolution of e-business. *Exceptional Customer Service* is not only a must-read, it's a must-use book that should not sit on the bookshelves of corporate libraries. It should be on the desk of managers and frontline associates for ready reference during team meetings, training sessions, and in the heat of battle with challenging customers.

We hope you enjoy the book, but, moreover, we hope you use it! And remember—today is a great day to get started.

—Lisa, David, and Bill

A Great Day to Get Started

"It's a GREAT day at Gerald's Tires! My name is Scott, how may I help you?"

This is the unmistakable, enthusiastic greeting you will receive when you call Gerald's Tires in Charleston, South Carolina. We begin this book by telling you a little of Gerald's story for a couple of reasons.

First, we want you to know about them because they represent the true essence of creating the *customer experience*. Secondly, we like Gerald's because everyone can relate to them—both as a customer and as a service professional.

BULLSEYE

They are not Walt Disney World, Nordstrom, Ritz-Carlton, or FedEx—the names you so often hear associated with exceptional customer care. They are a simple tire and brake store with five locations and fewer than 70 employees. They deliver what many perceive to be a commodity product in a competitive industry, and yet they have distinguished themselves as Service Stars. The best part about getting to know Gerald's is that you can see that what they have is not magic, nor is it perfection. What they have is an organizational culture that never loses sight of the customer. Almost never anyway—and in this world that puts them in the top .00001 percent!

Meet Bill Watts, the president, and David Ard, Gerald's vice president and general manager. Better yet, meet Scott Cook, Jane, Andy, Amy, or any of the 67 employees and you will walk away impressed! These folks have such a simple philosophy—make the customer happy! In fact, it's such a simple philosophy, you almost don't realize the planning and systems that make their customer care program work so well.

Through meeting the team at Gerald's, you will understand the company's "makes sense" approach as to how to create the *total customer experience*. From there, this book will give you more examples, exercises, and tools to impact your individual and team customer care skills.

How It All Began

When you do business with Gerald's Tires, you might expect there to be someone named Gerald. It must be the owner, right? *Wrong*. Well, maybe half right, there was someone named Gerald, but he wasn't always the owner. The business began when two men, Howard Watts and John Sullivan, decided to carve out a niche in the tire industry by opening a retread-only tire store. Gerald Davis was a deliveryman working for Howard at his retread manufacturing plant. When the company opened its first retail retread store, Gerald was given the opportunity to run it. He greeted the folks, changed the tires, exchanged the cash, and was even known to dispense some personal advice now and then. The store's original owners, Howard Watts and John Sullivan, thought it might be a good idea to name the store after the man who represented the business so well each and every day—Gerald. And was that one proud employee! Gerald ran the store like he owned it; he treated the customers like he owned it. And guess what. Customers treated Gerald like he owned it, too. In fact, as the business grew, Gerald became part owner of four stores. Gerald's legacy for personal service lives on today at these fine stores.

Inspiration with a Plan

So how do the current owners and managers of Gerald's keep the service spirit alive? How do they retain their employees at levels far above industry standards? Why is it their customers keep coming back and they tell their friends and neighbors to do the same? We'll tell you why. They have a plan. They would never call it a plan, but that's just what it is. It's a system that begins with employee recruitment and training. It's a system that stays healthy through continuous measurement of results; and it promotes itself with attitude, communication, and a determination to always do what's in the best interest of the customer.

How They Hire

If you want a job at Gerald's, be prepared to take a personality test. A personality test to change tires? You bet. Every employee at Gerald's is screened for his or her social interaction skills. Sure, they look for organization, attention to detail, and other professional traits, but above all else, they'll sacrifice some "dotting of i's and crossing of t's" to get a person who relates well to other people. They want a person who not only enjoys people but who enjoys *serving* other people.

And once they find the right person they train them. Is it formal training of *x*-hours in a classroom? No. Are they required to take tests? No. But the training is important, and the company's expectations are clear. Here are a few examples:

Phone Skills: Gerald's recognizes the importance of telephone skills in their dealings with customers. The telephone is often the first impression made, and it's an opportunity to reinforce relationships throughout the customer experience. At Gerald's they have a script. It's very specific. It tells you just how to answer the phone, how to use your name, how to ask for the customer's name, how many times to use the customer's name, and how many times to use the store's name. Yet with all of this, the script is flexible enough to allow an employee to inject his or her personality into the call. It is anything but robotic.

Policy Stomping: Gerald's coaches employees on certain words to use (or not use) that reflect their company's culture. For example, you better not hear an employee talk about "company policy." Customers don't want to hear about policy. Think about it. When do you usually encounter the word policy? It's most often being used defensively in some sort of service standoff. Rather than citing policy, isn't it better to ask the customer what they would expect in the situation or, simply put, what would make them happy or what do they believe is fair?

Customer Recovery: Bill Watts, president, is the first to admit that Gerald's slips now and then. But the company doesn't take those slips lightly, and when they do occur, they are ready to make it right. Bill spends a great deal of his time coaching employees on *doing what's right for the customer*. "Don't call me," he says. "I'm not standing there with the customer. I'm not looking at his car, and listening to his concerns. You are. You have good judgement. Just do what you think is best." End of lesson.

Measuring the Customer Experience: Gerald's uses three different techniques for keeping abreast of their customers' opinions.

1. Mystery shoppers and teleshoppers—hiring "fake" customers to do business with your stores and report on their findings.
2. In-store comment cards.
3. Follow-up phone calls to make sure everything was OK.

On a day when I visited Bill at his office (a place he'd rather not be if he can spend time with folks at his stores) he grabbed a stack of comment cards from his in basket. We flipped through them together to see just what customers were saying about their experiences. I was stunned. The comment cards have a rather typical rating scale of 1 to 10, representing poor to excellent. They ask for impressions regarding prompt greeting, courtesy, wait time, etc. What I saw was 10, 10, 10, 10, 10, 10, 10! Rarely did a customer give any other rating. And when asked if they'd recommend Gerald's to a friend, not only did customers check yes, but they often wrote in, "already do." Now there's a loyal following!

Bill relayed a funny story where one gentleman wrote in on six different comment cards, "You need more benches outside." What a nice problem to have—not enough benches for all the customers waiting. As you would expect, more benches were ordered, but so was something else. Gerald's sent the commenting gentleman a gift basket with a personal note that said, *"We heard you about the benches. Come visit us and try them out. Thanks as always for your business."*

And Then Some

The overall philosophy at Gerald's is give 'em what they ask for, *and then some!* In other words, don't just handle the transaction, build a relationship. Maybe it's just a southern way of saying, "exceed their expectations!" One thing for sure, it works. The employees understand it, and the customers appreciate it.

One of the "and then somes" that Gerald's is most noted for is giving a rose to every female customer. It is laid on the seat of each car before pickup, and it comes with a note that expresses special appreciation for the business. Gerald's knows how intimidating car service stations can be for people, and they are constantly striving to soften the rough edges.

Pass Me the Silver Bullet

Bill is frequently requested to speak to college students, trade groups, and at various industry forums about Gerald's' service success. He reluctantly agrees. And when he does, he's quick to point to the other

66 associates in the company that make it what it is. And finally he says, *"There is no silver bullet for service. People keep looking for it. Is it the roses, the enthusiasm, the personality-based recruiting, or the countless other 'and then somes'? Maybe yes, maybe no, maybe partly. But it is the culmination of many little things—all of which are delivered with a smile."*

Nothing More than Survival

This book is about customer service—nothing more, nothing less. This book is also about competitiveness, profitability, and, in fact, business survival. Nothing more, nothing less. The two are really one and the same, and owners like Bill Watts know it. There are plenty of very good tire stores in Charleston, South Carolina. Plenty of places to go if service at Gerald's takes a nosedive.

Consider the reasons why customers go elsewhere. A number of surveys have been done on the subject including this one a few years ago reported by the American Society for Quality and the Quality and Productivity Center. Here's what it showed:

Why Companies Lose Customers	
Customer dies	1%
Customer moves away	3%
Customer influenced by friends	5%
Customer lured away by competition	9%
Customer dissatisfied with product	14%
Customer turned away by an attitude of indifference on part of service provider	**68%**

That's right! Sixty-eight percent of the time that your business loses a customer it's because of poor service—a rude or indifferent attitude. If that statistic alone isn't a wake-up call, consider this one. The average company loses half of its customers every five years and doesn't even know it lost them, much less the reasons why. You do the math on what impact that has on the bottom line of your business.

As If That Wasn't Enough

Here are a few more statistics to consider:

★ It costs between five and six times more to attract a new customer than to keep an existing one.

★ According to research done by Bain & Company, companies can boost profits anywhere from 25 to 125 percent by retaining merely 5 percent more existing customers.

★ A 2 percent increase in customer retention has the same effect on profits as cutting costs by 10 percent.

★ Happy customers tell 4 to 5 others of their positive experience. Dissatisfied customers tell 9 to 12 how bad it was.

★ A study by Daniel Yankolovich revealed that two-thirds of customers do not feel valued by those serving them.

You may have seen some of these numbers before, or other studies with slightly different results. From looking at these numbers, two messages are crystal clear:

1. Exceptional customer service results in greater customer retention, which in turn results in higher profitability.
2. Most organizations haven't gotten that message yet or are ignoring it if they have.

Just Wait Until Next Week

A case in point: Not too long ago, a *New York Times* reader named Dorothy Klein sent a story into the Metropolitan Diary section of the paper, a weekly feature about life in New York City. In the story, Ms. Klein described the scene at a large post office in Brooklyn where a long line of customers was not so patiently waiting for service. Only one window was open and the wait seemed endless. All at once, five postal workers appeared carrying a ladder, balloons, and a banner that read "Customer Appreciation Week." Slowly the workers proceeded to hang the banner. Meanwhile, the line of customers barely moved. Finally, a very frustrated man near the end of the line pointed out to the supervisor that while five workers were hanging a customer appreciation banner, people had been waiting for more than half an hour for service because only one window was open. He asked the manager, "Do you not see an inconsistency here?" "Oh that," she replied, glancing at the banner and at her work crew, "that doesn't start until next week."

Haven't we all experienced this type of situation somewhere, sometime? Or we walk into a store and immediately see a sign that reads something like, *"Through these doors pass the most important people on earth—our customers!"* Thirty minutes later, after searching desperately, you finally find a sales associate. Apparently, many businesses think that by simply *declaring* dedication to the customer that behavior will magically follow. Unfortunately, it doesn't happen that way. It takes more than words and even more than the right attitude toward customers. Exceptional customer care takes a plan, a method of translating attitude into action. Bill Watts has a plan at Gerald's—it includes recruitment, training, feedback, measurement, and many other service aspects.

It's All in the Attitude

In the following chapters of this book we will discuss various parts of that service plan. We'll talk about attitude of service providers and the important role it plays in service excellence. The human resource firm HrEasy Inc. recently surveyed 1,000 applicants for customer service associate jobs. The results were very revealing.

* ★ 41 percent disagreed with the statement that the customer is always right.
* ★ 25 percent said it is hard to keep a positive attitude when dealing with customers.

★ 20 percent felt most customers were too demanding.
★ Finally, and sadly, 15 percent said that dealing with customers gets in the way of getting their job done.

Yes, you heard it right, 15 percent of a sample of 1,000 people applying to serve the public feel that the customer gets in the way. We've always heard the tongue-in-cheek lament of harried associates that this would be a nice place to work if we just didn't have to deal with customers, but this survey reports that many are actually serious about that statement! Imagine that! If I just didn't have those long lines of people and cars, imagine how many hamburgers I could make!

Business to Business

Many of the stories and examples we use in the book are retail businesses—restaurants, hotels, airlines, department stores, etc. We use a lot of them because most of us can relate personally to the good and bad examples of service. We've witnessed it. The principles of exceptional customer service apply equally in business-to-business situations, however. Supply chain management, as it is often called, involves the numerous and complex relationships necessary to fuel today's economy. Whether it's an automobile or airplane manufacturer relying on thousands of parts suppliers; a busy legal or accounting firm dependent on office machine and computer maintenance; or a hospital in need of fresh linens, quality food, and smooth working relationships with doctors' offices and health maintenance organizations; customer care is vital. In each of these examples, one or more customer-supplier relationships exists, and the nature of competition is such that business customers will "walk" just as quickly if service is poor as you and I do if we are treated rudely at a restaurant.

Lincoln Contractors Supply Company in Milwaukee, Wisconsin, a supplier of industrial hardware, understands this. They also understand the need for a plan. Ten years ago, the company implemented a "Customer for Life" business philosophy. They look at every customer and ask, "How much could this person or company spend with us over the course of their lifetime?" Lincoln doesn't want to deal with a customer just once, you see, they want a customer's business forever.

The company has more than just a vision, however. It has a *plan* to accomplish that vision, a plan that involves creating an atmosphere where the customer says "Wow." Here are a few things Lincoln does:

★ Maintains large, clean showrooms with 20,000 items on display. Showrooms are maintained professionally and attractively.

★ Thinks of the store as a home and customers as guests. That means cookies in the showroom in the morning, pretzels in the afternoon, coffee and tea, and 25-cent sodas in the soft drink machine (many contractors come in for their quarter soda and end up buying something). On hot summer days, a five-gallon cooler full of Gatorade is also available at the counter.

★ Encourages the sales staff always to try and exceed customer expectations. When dealing with a challenging customer, they are told to ask the customer what is fair, then take it one step or a few dollars further—in the customer's favor.

Lincoln Industrial Supply gets it, just like Gerald's gets it. They understand customers and customer service. They have only one rule for the entire workforce:

Empower your people to make decisive and
immediate customer service decisions.

Teams, TQM, and Service

One final thought before moving on. The concepts of teams and team-work have fallen into disfavor in some quarters over the past few years. Teams have become closely linked to many of the management fads of the last 25 years, such as quality circles, total quality management, self-directed work teams, and others. It's not that any of those programs were bad. On the contrary, many of these concepts were instrumental in helping to rekindle America's productivity and competitiveness during the second half of the last century.

Where programs such as TQM fell short, in the view of many executives, was that they were treated as business objectives in and of themselves. Lori Silverman, a nationally recognized expert on organization development and author of *Critical Shift: The Future of Quality in Organizational Performance*, says that quality has gone into hiding. In this new millennium, companies are emphasizing total operational management and creating value for employees, consumers, shareholders, and society. In Silverman's view, this creation of value involves a lot more than quality management concepts. It means total obsession with customer needs, alignment of all work with mission, vision, and values, and a commitment to social and community responsibility.

What's the point? Teams and teamwork remain a vital part of business strategy, particularly in the area of customer care. As you read on in this book, you will see that maintaining a positive attitude 40 or more hours a week is hard. You will learn that as a frontline associate, *you don't always have all the answers* to your customers' questions and problems. Finally, you will hear about Service Stars and how important the customer service team is to their individual performance.

As you read the pages that follow and do the exercises that we have included, keep the team concept in mind. Regardless of the type of organization, its size, or the product or service delivered, remember that as a customer care associate, you are not alone. Rely not only on your own ability, experience, and attitude, but draw on the strengths of your coworkers as together you serve your customers.

It's a Wrap

Did you catch all of the following points?

The Gerald's Tire story
- ★ A "plan" for maintaining service levels
- ★ The "people connection"
  - • Hire people who want to serve others
  - • Train, train, train
- ★ Emphasize the basics
  - • Telephone skills—the first line of communication
  - • It's our policy—NOT!
  - • Customer recovery—do what's right!
  - • Measure customer happiness

Customer satisfaction "by the numbers"
- ★ Sixty-eight percent of customers go elsewhere due to attitude
- ★ Customers . . . it costs more to get 'em than keep 'em
- ★ Unhappy customers tell nine to 12 others . . . and who knows how many on the Internet?
- ★ Fifteen percent of applicants for service positions say customers get in the way!

Don't forget business-to-business/customer-supplier relationships

The customer service team
- ★ Rely on your fellow associates
- ★ You don't have all the answers

Aerobicize Your Program: Why Everyone Isn't Doing Customer Service

The term *customer service* is losing its punch. It's sad, but true. Be careful that you don't misunderstand what was just said. The term is losing its punch, not the act, or better yet, the impact. Customer service is no less important in today's marketplace than at any other time. In fact, the need for improved customer service is at an all-time high. Why? Because of the changing ways in which we conduct business. Why? Because consumers have increasingly more choices. Why? Because customers have lower levels of brand and product loyalty. Think about it. How differently is your organization doing business today than it did just five years ago?

★ Most organizations are flatter with fewer levels of management.
★ Teams and self-led work groups are becoming more prevalent.
★ Technology, most notably e-commerce, is transforming communications, order, and delivery systems, radically redefining our markets.

The list goes on, but the real dilemma is: if customer service is so important, then why aren't more businesses doing it well? The National Quality Research Center at the University of Michigan reports in its American Customer Satisfaction Index that customer satisfaction has been declining about one percentage point per year. In fact, in the most recent annual survey, customers claimed a satisfactory experience in only 73 out of 100 shopping events. The good news is that this figure is up from 72 in 1999. The bad news? Consumers are not satisfied with product or service 27 times out of 100!

Consider a Typical Morning

To illustrate the poor service that we consumers are subjected to, I have chronicled a typical weekday morning. Actually it's less than two hours of a morning. You may confront many of the same type of experiences in your day. What a sad state of affairs I have to report.

Tuesday, 6:40 A.M. Before starting my usual workday routine, I decide to take care of some of the less pleasurable tasks that have to be done. For example, I received a bill in the mail from my previous cellular telephone provider. The bill was for one dollar. No explanation, just one dollar. I was puzzled by the bill since I had called to terminate the service more than two months prior, but I also knew it wouldn't go away by itself. My first thought was this was some quirky overage in the balance, and I should just pay it and be done. While usually opting to take the easy road, something nagged me about this and I decided to place a call to the 1-800 service number. It was a 24-hour number, which I liked. It was just before 7:00 A.M. I wasn't prepared for what followed.

After a seemingly interminable wait (how many people could be calling at 6:50 A.M. EST?) cluttered with all sorts of recorded marketing messages and music, a customer care representative named Greg finally answered my call. Greg was able to explain the charge quite simply. This was a monthly fee to be paid for having my phone "on suspension." Oh, so that's the problem—somehow they thought my phone was suspended, not disconnected. Easy to fix? Not so fast, Ace.

Greg was happy to terminate my phone service as of today but didn't seem to grasp that I had called to terminate it 63 days earlier. He did show a record of my original call but held his ground that I had requested a suspension, not termination. I was just shy of feeling like Greg didn't believe me—like I was trying to sham them for a dollar. "Now let's not be silly. Let it drop. We are only talking a dollar," I thought to myself for a minute. Of course that wasn't the point. For me, it was the principle involved. Greg said he had no way of waiving the one-dollar fee. Hard to believe, so I asked for a supervisor. None was available, but I could leave a number and be assured that someone would call me back. Enough was enough. I told Greg to terminate the service once and for all and that I would promptly send a check for the ridiculous one dollar.

At this point, some hint of past training triggered in Greg's mind. He asked me if I had already selected another cellular provider and if there was anything he could do to keep my business. "Oh no," I assured him, "the decision is final, and I think it's a good one."

As I hung up the phone, many thoughts ran through my head. Did the company so frown on terminations that the original representative purposely coded it as a suspension? Was it a simple entry mistake on the first representative's part? If it was a mistake, were there not policies for correcting it so as to please the customer? Why was I not asked on the first call how my business could be retained? Did they know this was a pricing issue? Did they think I was moving? Was it quality of service or product? There was so much to be learned in this relatively minor interaction, and yet no one cared enough to take initiative. One thing was for sure, it said to me that the company really didn't care about my business.

7:10 A.M. You won't believe the next call I made. This call was to my new cellular provider. You see, I couldn't find my mobile phone that morning when leaving the house. I usually kept it in my car, and after a thorough search of house and car, I concluded that it might have been stolen. I almost never lock my car.

Anyway, now I'm dialing another customer care center to report the loss and check on my insurance coverage. Great! A real person answered the call on the second ring. Brenda was pleasant and clear in her greeting. I congratulated myself again for having switched to this company. Uh-oh. Things suddenly started sliding downhill. First I was informed that I did not have insurance on my phone. Although I was sure I had requested it when I bought the phone, the fact was they had no record. Brenda seemed quite eager at that point to sell me a new insurance plan for my account (I couldn't help but think she had a sales quota to meet). The problem was we weren't addressing the issue that my phone was missing. I had no phone to insure. Wasn't this somehow backwards? Without boring you with the dialogue in between, we decided it was best to suspend my service until I found my phone or purchased a new one. Again the thoughts began popping in my head. How was it that I didn't have insurance from the get-go? While I could understand not being able to reinstate it retroactively, I did at least want some sympathy and recognition that this may have been their error, not mine. In the end I found my phone and added the insurance option. The company has dropped an unfortunate notch on my scale.

7:40 A.M. In somewhat disbelief, I realized that almost an hour had passed. Now I'm rushed for an 8:00 A.M. appointment in town. All the traffic lights were in my favor and the day was looking up, until I pulled into the garage of the office complex where I was meeting. The garage was dark and dirty and had extremely tight aisles and spaces. I drove in circles for what seemed like 10 levels before finding a space. COMPACT CAR ONLY. I guess that meant it didn't want my sport utility truck. I'd have parked in it anyway if I thought it would fit. So back down the levels I go until I finally encounter a garage attendant. "I'm running late, where can I park this thing?" I blurted as I slowed to a stop. "We're pretty full," he responded. "Don't know what to tell ya." Obviously he didn't. He might as well have said, "Tough!" I wanted to hear things like "Pull over here in this reserved spot. I know she's on vacation." Or, "Leave your keys with me, and I'll find a suitable space. You can pick the keys up at the ticket booth when you return." How about, "I'm sorry this is making you late. I'll be glad to call the person you're meeting and tell them you're having trouble finding parking in our garage."

The potential responses are many. The problem is that we often don't consider the impact to the customer. Consider that this is a "professionals" building, meaning it houses lawyers, accountants, a bank, and a brokerage firm. What impressions are being made on their behalf? How easy are you finding it to do business with them? Do you feel safe? Does the experience make you want to return?

The Answer Is Simple

We ask again. If customer care is so vital to the success, not to mention survival of a company, then why aren't more organizations doing it well? The answer is simple, but the implementation is not. Delivering exceptional customer care takes a plan, a commitment, and training, training, training! You see, developing an exceptional customer service program is much like developing a fitness routine. It's a workout; it's aerobics. It's not a one-time grueling workout. It's a long-term program of constant activity. After all, you don't talk about running to become a marathon runner. You are not simply inspired to become an Olympic swimmer. If you truly understand the positive impacts of a distinguishing service program, then you must work at it constantly and consistently.

Searching for Solutions

Delivering exceptional customer care doesn't just happen. You are dealing with issues that span the entire breadth and depth of the organization. From corporate policies to phone systems to facility appearance to personal appearance, dress, tone, listening skills, energy, manners—it all can be overwhelming. Don't let it be. Follow these steps:

★ Identify your primary points of customer contact.
★ Examine the goals you want to accomplish for your customers.

★ Determine the type of people skills and technology functions needed to accomplish those goals.
★ Construct a plan that provides the tools needed to do the job well, including a well-defined training program.

Notes

Note to team members: It may sound as if the above solutions need to be directed to management. After all, how much impact can be made at the frontline by customer care teams? Plenty! Do not read these and begin pointing fingers at management. Empower yourselves to take a look at aspects of the customer relationship that you can control and take action, or at the very least, make recommendations.

Studies have reported that well over 90 percent of all customer service problems can be directly linked to managerial issues. Read carefully, we said *managerial* not *management* issues. The difference is that *managerial* relates to HOW an issue is being addressed or managed. A *management* issue describes WHO is addressing it. An individual employee, and certainly teams, can have significant impact on *managerial* issues. To further illustrate the difference, here's a true story that happened while dining out recently.

We walked into a neighborhood eatery with some friends. It's a fun, casual place—not expensive but not cheap. We were seated by a hostess we knew from previous visits. She always had a warm smile and cheerful greeting. She apologized for the short wait and put us at a table in the center of the room beneath a ceiling fan. It didn't take long before we all started to comment on the cool temperatures and the breeze of the fan. By the time our waiter approached, we were shivering. Offering help immediately, he brought a stool over so that he could reach the cord on the ceiling fan to turn it off. *(Turning off the fan was a managerial issue.)* We were grateful, and this helped, but only temporarily. You see, there was a large air vent nearby that was blowing arctic air directly on our table. And it wasn't just us. We noticed others in the restaurant with cold arms crossed and sweaters pulled over. When we asked our waiter if he could adjust the thermostat, he sheepishly said he couldn't. You see, the restaurant owner kept a lockbox on the main thermostat *(this is a management issue)*. Now what sense did this make? Was he trying to control costs? Did he not trust his employees? Since he was absent most evenings, what possibly could have led him to this decision? Nonetheless, damage was done. When we think of that restaurant now, we think of ice cubes and padlocks.

When you confront management issues that frustrate you, take notice of how many are tied to cost savings. It would serve many an organization well if they took notes from Jan Carlzon, former president of Scandinavian Airlines Systems. He said, "What's the danger of giving away too much? Are you worried about having an over-satisfied customer? That is not much of a worry. You can forget about an over-satisfied customer because an unsatisfied customer is one of the most expensive problems you can have. The danger is not that employees will give away too much. It's that they won't give away anything because they don't dare."

The Ritz-Carlton Hotel Company certainly understands this philosophy. As a recognized worldwide leader in their industry, they are continually shattering records for distinguishing service. All employees in their organization have a $2,000 spending authority to use for the sole purpose of "moving heaven and earth" to satisfy a customer. This is called *empowering* the employees. This type of devotion to the customer does not happen accidentally. It's a culture that is lived and taught at all levels. The hotel's president, Horst Schulze, takes an active role in setting this standard of care. For him, they are not selling rooms and food, they are selling service!

An idea at Marriott Hotels costs very little, and it makes a tremendous statement. Marriott has put together a *Sweet Dreams* package. It consists of a small bud vase, a flower, and some homemade cookies. Hotel staff members are encouraged to give it to customers who are having difficulties that the hotel really can't fix. For example, a guest enters the hotel complaining that she's tired, feels awful, and her four-hour plane delay didn't help. That's the cue for the staff person to send this guest a *Sweet Dreams*. While the hotel couldn't control the circumstances regarding this guest's day, they could control how they responded to it. And better yet, when one employee noticed a guest with an awful cough, a box of cough drops was included with the *Dreams* package. Now that's exceptional service! Don't think for a minute that customer loyalty and word-of-mouth advertising haven't paid for that box of cough drops.

By George, I Think He's Got It

Can you stand another hotel story? They are such havens for service delivery. This one was told to me while working with a senior executive group at a property in Virginia. This group had a financial consultant working with them, and hence he was a guest in the hotel one evening. The consultant was a runner. He'd gone out that morning for his early run, came back in, and wanted to get a newspaper. Since the complimentary copies at the front desk were gone, he went by the gift shop, where there was a stack of papers by the door. Since the shop hadn't opened yet, he leaned over, picked up one of the papers, walked about 12 feet back to the front desk, and said, "I've picked up one of your papers—here's 50 cents." And the person at the front desk said, "No, I can't do that. We're two different departments, and I don't have any way to enter that into my system." Okay. He puts his 50 cents back in his pocket, puts the paper back, and walks on. He happens upon a guy cleaning out the fireplace (a houseman) who's preparing the big fire in the lobby for the day. The consultant says to him, "I know the coffee shop's not open yet. Do you know where I can get a cup of coffee?" And the houseman says, "Sure, how do you take it?" "Black." "I'll be right back." The houseman goes away, comes back in a few moments with a piping hot cup of black coffee in a styrofoam cup. "I'll be working around here for at least the next 20 minutes. When you need a refill, let me know."

Does this guy get it or what? He obviously feels empowered. Now contrast the two employees. The front desk clerk was faced with something that she didn't know how to bend the rules on. If you were working that front desk, don't you think that you would have stood there and said: Now wait a minute. Gift shop's not open, but he just gave me 50 cents. When Christine opens up the gift shop, I'll just holler over there and say, "Christine, I've got 50 cents for one of the papers. Here." Does that make sense? Of course it does, but you'd be amazed how many employees don't feel comfortable in stepping outside of their box of rules.

Things You Can Do to Make a Difference!

★ Think of a situation where you have felt limited by company policy or procedure in serving your customer.

★ Ask your team leader what specific freedoms you have to go beyond this policy.

★ Substitute yourself for the last customer you served. Would you have been satisfied with the service? Would you have felt the experience was exceptional in any way?

★ What's one thing you will do to make a difference in the service provided with your next customer?

Note to team leader: Have you tried calculating the cost of a lost customer? Have you tracked the cost of implementing some extra service ideas or upgrades? Compare these costs and take them to your team and to upper management.

Training Is Sustaining

Let's begin by establishing what we mean by training. Training comes in many shapes and sizes. It is informal and formal. It's introductory and refresher. It can be fun and participative. It can be grueling and intense. It is an investment, not a cost. Most importantly, training must be ongoing!

At Lands' End, a customer care representative receives 75 hours of initial training before he or she is allowed to answer the first call. At FedEx, new employees receive five weeks of training with refresher courses every four months. And at Walt Disney World, no employee is allowed to begin work within the theme park until he or she has completed three weeks of education. As for the folks at Ritz-Carlton, they estimate that an average of $2,700 to $3,500 is spent training each employee. And guess what—their turnover is 40 percent below industry standards. Numerous examples can be cited, but just consider this league of companies that invest in training. These companies know that it's the quality of their workforce and the appreciation of the customer that sustains their business growth. They know that employee training is one of their better investments.

At Target, a national discount retailer, employee turnover among hourly associates was a staggering 89 percent in 1989. They were able to whittle that down in a little more than two years to 59 percent. They did that by creating Target University. This university truly gives people skills, ways to deal with difficult customers, and ways to deal with some of the stressful situations that they can find themselves in. Basically, they are equipping people emotionally to handle the frontline. They are not just teaching them how to run cash registers and stock inventory. And guess what? In addition to decreasing turnover, Target also experienced increased customer satisfaction scores during the same period.

Many large companies have in-house learning centers such as Target University. We like the name *learning center* because it conveys the benefit to the employee, as opposed to training center, which merely describes the function that is being performed. At many of these organizations, becoming a trainer is quite an accomplishment. Training positions are highly sought, compensated well, and command the respect of fellow associates and top management.

Learning centers are excellent, but they can have their drawbacks as well. They may tend to centralize and formalize the training function such that information is not as relevant and easy to access as it should be. By their very nature, learning centers also can become stale and canned in their material and presentation. Think about it. Shouldn't learning be integrated into everyday activities as much as possible? This is where employee teams have a distinct advantage. You can take the initiative to include training snippets into each and every team meeting. Plan to set aside 10 minutes of each team meeting to discuss a service-related event or issue. This can be as simple as reviewing a very positive service event and what specifically made the difference to the customer. You could rotate the responsibility with a different person responsible each week for bringing an article of service to the meeting for discussion. Be creative, but be disciplined. Don't let this be the last item that gets squeezed off the meeting agenda. If you do, you will have said a great deal about where you place service training in your priorities. This can be a fun and productive way of involving all team members in honing their customer care skills. There is more about this in Chapter 12.

Make Training Fun

When most people are asked to describe their impressions of training, they use words such as *boring, long, dated,* and *tiring.* Well it needn't be. Training can and should be fun, interactive, and full of challenges. At Target University they play some pretty crazy games. They have characters called Bad Mouth Betty and Hysterical Harold. At another company, they have Lowball Larry and Rude Rudy as part of their sales and service training. The challenge is to script these characters to the extreme in role-play situations so that trainees have a chance to use their skill at dealing with the somewhat outrageous. Having participated in some of these sessions, I can tell you they are full of laughter and learning.

In order to reinforce the continuous learning concept, a computer company has adopted a unique idea. Each Friday the employees put on a T-shirt that has "Well Trained" printed on the front. On the back of the shirt there is a checklist of all the training courses offered by the company. A check by the course indicates the employee's successful completion of the course. It has become a real badge of honor to wear these shirts. The sales force for this company has a seven-week curriculum. It touches on everything from products to the order entry. They also have courses that put them in the shoes of the customer so they can empathize with the buyers' needs and wants. As new and still inexperienced trainees, they are given a brand new box with a computer as it is shipped from the plant. They must open it, unpack it, install all programs, and have it ready to go. Tell me this doesn't build empathy for the customer. And the learning doesn't stop there. The trainees observe customer calls to get a feel for the type of issues they will confront. They analyze these calls and learn from them. Can you imagine how service would improve if more companies had this type of training program?

Training does work. But remember, when you are developing customer care skills, you are most likely talking about changing individual behavior. That takes times. It takes repetition. It takes consistency of message and continual reinforcement. Sounds like a fitness program doesn't it? And like an aerobics workout, try stopping for several weeks and then jumping back in. You will be amazed at how quickly you become out of shape.

Following is an exercise that incorporates a number of the points covered in this chapter:

★ Identifying direct and indirect customer contact opportunities
★ Generating fresh ideas for service enhancement
★ How to use team meetings as mini training sessions

Allow 20 minutes per exercise below.

Exercise

HOW FIT IS YOUR ORGANIZATION?

A. Make a list of the points of customer contact within your organization. These may be face-to-face, phone, and/or written contacts such as letters, invoices, agreements, etc. Have each team member select a different point of contact where possible.

B. Each member is to monitor/observe or review one point of contact and make notes as to how that contact could have been more customer focused. (Duplicate this page as needed.)

C. Bring the above observations to your next team meeting. Have at least two or three examples and recommendations shared. Follow this with open discussion as to how that contact could have been improved.

D. Don't stop here. Vote on the best ideas and see what you can do to make the necessary changes. It may be in the form of a recommendation/suggestion to management or a team-led implementation. Do your best to determine cost and timeline for implementation. Take ownership!

Contact Type	What You Observed	Suggestions

It's a Wrap

Did you catch all of the following points?

Customer service is more important than ever
★ Consumers—the choice is theirs (and they have a lot!)
★ Brand and product loyalty isn't what it used to be
★ Technology and e-business are turning marketplaces upside down
★ Nobody told the service providers—73 percent customer satisfaction rating in this country

The Service Workout Program
★ It doesn't just happen—you need a plan
★ Management versus managerial issues—there's a difference
★ Put the *power* into em*power*ment
★ How can you make a difference for a customer?

Training is sustaining
★ An investment with high return
★ Do it often and make it fun
★ Don't stop or you'll get out of shape

The Plot Thickens: Learning to Plot Your Path to Service Stardom

Picture this. You're strolling along on a beautiful summer evening. You've just finished a relaxing dinner, and you happen upon an ice cream shoppe. This isn't just any ice cream store. It's top of the line (hence the extra "pe" on "shop"). They have more flavors and fancy names than you could imagine. The store is bright and cheery in its design and there's a sweet smell in the air. It makes your mouth water. The large array of cones is lined up before you at the counter, from plain to sugar and a variety of flavored waffle cones! You are ready to indulge.

Now the bubble bursts. The first person you confront behind the counter has made it clear you are not her priority. She makes no effort to

finish a phone conversation, one that is quite obviously personal. As she hangs up and stands before you, you feel compelled to ask, "Are you ready to take my order?" As you begin, a young man crashes through the swinging door at the back of the shoppe—you are thinking FIRE!—then he rushes to the front door, props it open, and begins to hurl the sidewalk cafe furniture indoors in preparation for closing. You look at your watch and notice it's 7:43 P.M. "What an odd time to close," you think.

You get your waffle cone anyway and sit inside the shoppe to enjoy it. Out comes a mop and bucket of ammonia water, as employee number three begins to wash the floors while you try to enjoy your dessert. Ahh, the taste of Chocolate *Ammonia* Mint in a hazelnut cone! But being a good customer, you merely continue eating your ice cream while remembering to raise your feet as employee number three mops beneath your table. OK, you say to yourself, you've had enough and you walk out. At least you can enjoy the ice cream in the pleasant night air. Just as you're crossing the store's threshold, you hear the counter girl shout to employees two and three, "I'm covering the ice cream now. Tell anyone that walks in that we aren't serving anymore." You check your watch. It's 7:54 P.M. You shake your head and leave.

If Only It Weren't True

This is a small example of the clueless nature by which so many businesses operate. Did any of these thoughts come to mind as you read the tale of the ice cream shoppe?

 ★ I wonder what the owner would think about this situation?
 ★ What a shame I have no desire to go back there even though the ice cream was delicious.
 ★ You just can't find good help these days.
 ★ Will these kids ever understand the meaning of work ethic?
 ★ I wonder how long they will be in business?
 ★ Who's in charge here anyway? Is there no manager?
 ★ I wish I could get that ammonia taste out of my mouth.

We could construct quite a list of reactions to such outrageous treatment. What is important here, however, is that we learn from this situation and the many like it that we encounter everyday.

The type of service experienced at our ice cream shoppe raises a lot of questions. Let's go through a *constructive* list of the issues and questions raised in this situation:

1. What type of hiring practices does the business utilize?
2. What type of training is given to employees before they begin work?
3. Have customer service expectations been made clear, and are they reinforced periodically?
4. Was a supervisor on the premises, and is a supervisor necessary?
5. Should the owner be present to monitor these activities?
6. What reward or recognition systems may have been in place to foster/encourage high levels of service?
7. Is there any method for customers to easily provide feedback on the service they received?
8. What would have been the reaction if something were said to these employees?
9. What procedures are in place to try and win back a disgruntled customer?
10. Have we quantified the extent of damage that poor service can do to future business and to profitability?

There can always be more questions or ideas to add, but this is the type of analysis that should take place. It is actually easier to do a constructive analysis with a situation we encounter rather than with situations where our customers encounter us. But don't let that deter you. This analysis needs to be done for every level of direct customer contact.

Notes

Squaring Off

You can begin to define your customer service program using a traditional scattergram tool. You can do this on many levels:

★ for you personally
★ for your company as a whole
★ for individual products or services provided by your company
★ for your competitors or industry as a whole

Let's first put some definition to the squares in the graph below along with some descriptive examples that illustrate ways to use it in your own planning. Then you can begin by categorizing activities and attributes of your company, your competition, and your personal work. That's right, your personal work. You should always attempt to personalize lessons of service right to your daily work activity.

It is interesting to observe that most companies have formal business plans. A great many also have periodic strategic plans, marketing plans, and some even have specific subplans such as a communication or public relations plans. Rarely, however, do you see a customer service plan. As critical as customer service is to a business, the absence of such a plan may be yet another indicator of a lack of commitment to truly serving the customer.

Consider the diagram on the next page.

Complacents (Low creativity, low implementation of ideas): Start with the lower left quadrant. This box represents the class of service providers that merely exist. They aren't rude or foreboding, yet they are not helpful

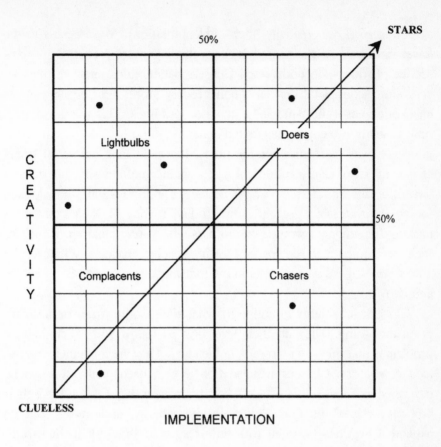

or necessarily pleasant either. They are part of the "HepYa" clan, the ones that stand behind counters and yell "Next" or "Canahhepya?"

Most likely they were never trained to serve or hired for their love of people, yet they are not rude or abusive as the Clueless can sometimes be. A good example of this is the robot-like cashier at the grocery store. You were greeted (you think), your products were scanned and bagged, and money was exchanged accurately. You may even have heard a "thanks." But never in the process did you feel special, appreciated, or cared for. And to think that he or she may have been your only contact with a human (representing the store, that is) throughout the entire grocery shopping experience.

Chasers (Low creativity, high implementation): Move across to the lower right box. As the name indicates, this is a more proactive group of service providers. To understand Chasers better, think again of the grocery store example. Consider when grocery stores first began express checkout lanes—the famous 12 items or less lines. This was a wonderfully fresh and welcome change that benefited the run-in shopper tremendously. It was innovative for the times. It wasn't long before all stores chased the idea. Can you think of a grocery store of any size that doesn't now offer this express service? It's no longer an innovation. If one looked for an innovation in grocery stores today, it may be their convenient parking for pregnant women or mothers with young children. It may be their electronic touch screens for locating specific products. Whatever the innovation—if it's a good one, know that the Chasers will soon pick up and copy it.

Chasers are highly attentive to what their competition or industry peers are doing. They do their level best to follow suit. Their biggest problem is that they are followers, not leaders. They are implementers, not idea generators. Chasers are also not very focused, and often can be described as "chasing their tails." For this reason they seldom leave their box of service influence. A lot of time, energy, and money can be expended by Chasers, often with little results to show for it. Beware of being caught in this box.

Lightbulbs (High creativity, low implementation of ideas): Shift now to the upper left quadrant. This is the idea box. Creativity and imagination surge here. Ever know those people who can come up with one good, fresh idea after another? The problem is the ideas rarely go anywhere. Just think how many times you and coworkers may have said, *"We should just try . . ."* or *"If they would just develop . . ."* or *"I don't understand why we don't start . . ."* These are "lightbulb" phrases. They usually indicate there is an idea out there, but it's floating. There is no true formulation, no owner, no one feeling empowered to take it and run.

Great ideas can come from most anywhere and anyone. But we are talking fresh, new ideas, not ideas copied from competitors. It is fair game, however, to get inspiration for a new feature or attribute from something similar in another industry, product line, or type of business. For example, several years ago an engineering firm was redoing their office filing system, which was in great disarray. They decided not only to purge or archive outdated files, but to reorganize and color code the remaining files for easy identification. Not only were they completely thrilled with the new system, but an idea was spawned from this. They began to think about color coding their reports to clients, which were very technical and lengthy and needed organization.

With one of those simple "ah-hahs," they were beginning to think how they could not only help their clients but also differentiate themselves from all of their competitors. No one in the industry was color-coding reports. Bing . . . the *lightbulb* illuminated.

Now let's take the next step. What if the workers stopped right there? After all, it wasn't within their scope to redesign a product. It would take all new printers and some new computers. How much would it cost? Who'd really benefit and how much? There can be such a litany of reasons not to proceed, but don't fall to these temptations. Better yet, build a structure for ideas not to wither, such as suggestion boxes with review teams or periodic creative sessions for ideas to be born and documented for follow-up.

If an idea merely flicks on a light and then it extinguishes, it's more of a firefly than a lightbulb. Can't you see a workplace full of fireflies with their tiny lights sparking on and off with the many good ideas? You don't want to be in an organization full of fireflies; you want good long-lasting lightbulbs.

An important reminder—lightbulbs should be turned off now and then. Not every idea will or should be pursued, but make sure the decision to turn off a lightbulb is a conscious one. Don't let them burn out or have others turn them off before their time.

Doers (High creativity...high implementation): Finally, move to the upper right quadrant. Now we are in the box of influence. Doers are as the name suggests. They are people and businesses of action, and they seek your business. They not only seek ways to improve their service to customers, they act on them. They are the products of planning and training. Think of the last time you crossed paths with a Doer.

★ How did you feel leaving the transaction?
★ Did you comment on it to someone?
★ Are you more likely to do business with them again?
★ Did the experience change your impression of the company?

I recently encountered a Doer. The saga began when I purchased shoes from a Bass Shoe Outlet Store while on vacation. I purchased two identical pairs, one black and one brown. I didn't take time to try on both pairs. I assumed that the boxes were marked correctly, and knowing my size, it seemed that trying on one pair was sufficient. Three weeks later I discovered I had a mixed pair—and a right shoe two sizes too large. I had thrown away the box and my receipt, and I was not looking forward to calling the store to plead for an exchange.

You see, my expectations were established and they weren't too high. It was my fault; I hadn't checked the shoes. I'd lost my receipt and the original box. The shoes were purchased out of town weeks before. And most of all, this is an outlet store. What did I really expect? Certainly not what I got.

A young man answered the phone and introduced himself as Jason. He quickly apologized for the mistake and assured me that it was the store's error, not mine. Employees are trained to check the shoes at the register to ensure correct merchandise, he said. The receipt and box were no problem. He asked if he could verify that they did have my correct shoe size in stock, and could he call me back. When I requested their address to ship my mixed breed back, he was quick to set up a UPS pickup so I wouldn't be troubled for the address or the expense. Needless to say, I was impressed. Thanks, Jason and Bass, for being such Doers!

Stars: At the very point of the arrow running through our scattergram are the *Service Stars*. This is the best of class. These are the organizations that consistently generate the bright new ideas and are able to see them through to implementation. They make their mark by being first with service innovations. Naturally, you can have individuals who are Stars (we devote an entire chapter to them later). You can have specific activities, products, or promotions that are Stars. The trick to being an organiza-

          X

STORE: 0521   REG: 02/88 TRAN#: 7306
SALE   02/07/2009 EMP: 00181
****

above and can be made for the same item only.

Periodicals, newspapers, comic books, food and drink, digital downloads, gift cards, return gift cards, items marked "non-returnable," "final sale" or the like and out-of-print, collectible or pre-owned items cannot be returned or exchanged.

Returns and exchanges to a Borders, Borders Express or Waldenbooks retail store of merchandise purchased from Borders.com may be permitted in certain circumstances. See Borders.com for details.

BORDERS.

Returns

Returns of merchandise purchased from a Borders, Borders Express or Waldenbooks retail store will be permitted only if presented in saleable condition accompanied by the original sales receipt or Borders gift receipt within the time periods specified below. Returns accompanied by the original sales receipt must be made within 30 days of purchase and the purchase price will be refunded in the same form as the original purchase. Returns accompanied by the original Borders gift receipt must be made within 60 days of purchase and the purchase price will be refunded in the form of a return gift card.

Exchanges of opened audio books, music, videos, video games, software and electronics will be permitted subject to the same time periods and receipt requirements as above and can be made for the same item only.

Periodicals, newspapers, comic books, food and drink, digital downloads, gift cards, return gift cards, items marked "non-returnable," "final sale" or the like and out-of-print, collectible or pre-owned items cannot be returned or exchanged.

Returns and exchanges to a Borders, Borders Express or Waldenbooks retail store of merchandise purchased from

tional Star is consistently having your people, activities, products, etc., also in the Star box. Be sure not to read too quickly over the word "consistently" in the previous sentence. Consistency is more important than frequency when it comes to being a Star. In other words, it is better to have three new ideas that are well planned and consistently implemented than to have ten new ideas of which several are partially or poorly implemented.

Stars can be found in today's world, but they are not plentiful. Do not fall into the trap of thinking Star organizations are always the high-priced leaders in an industry. For example, Nordstrom is definitely considered a Star. Ritz-Carlton is another Star organization. Not to take anything away from these fine corporations, but some might say, "They can afford to be Stars, have you seen what they charge?" This is simply a cop-out. They are Stars for many reasons that have nothing to do with their rates, and most importantly, Stars can be found in any organization, in any industry, with any product or service. Here are a couple of examples.

STAR EXAMPLE ONE: THE TALKING CAR

It was one of the South's dog days. Mid-August and my car's air-conditioning goes on the blink. Someone recommended a dealer close to my office, which certainly was convenient. From the minute I drove on their lot, I was impressed— clean, architecturally appealing, with very prompt and friendly service associates greeting me. I was served within minutes and then offered a ride back to the office in their shuttle. The driver couldn't have been nicer. He was a 17-year employee who mostly raved about how much he enjoyed his job. He was a proud employee who spoke volumes about his employer. While all of this was noticeably a step above other dealers, it wasn't Star material. But what happened next was *distinguishing*! When I picked up my car, I noticed a small card on the dash asking me to play the tape already inserted in my car's player. I dutifully followed instructions, and, boy, was I wowed. My service technician introduced himself and then proceeded to describe to me all that he did to my car. It was fairly detailed, but all in lay terms that I could easily understand. He then thanked me for bringing the car to him and encouraged me to call him directly if I had any questions whatsoever about my car's service. What can I say? I've told at least 50 people about this experience. Was the work performed any better than at another dealer? Probably not. Was the price better? I couldn't tell you. Would I return there again and would I recommend it to others? You bet!

STAR EXAMPLE TWO: THE GOURMET GARAGE

If ever there was a commodity, it's a city parking garage. After all, what's to differentiate? You enter, drive around in endless upward circles, park, pay, and leave. End of story, right? Wrong! Consider this special garage. Upon entering, the first thing you notice is the clean, bright colors and wide parking slots. Again, while that's nice, it's hardly Star material. But wait, as you exit your car, you hear Broadway show tunes being played —not too loud, not too soft. And here's the kicker—each floor has a different theme. The music and accompanying murals were different on each floor! A subtle yet unforgettable reminder where you parked your car. And they don't stop there. In the elevator are recorded messages telling you about the services of the garage. Need a wash, a wax, how about a quick vacuum? Just leave the keys with the attendant and your vehicle will be pampered to custom specifications. A commodity? I don't think so.

In Theodore Levitt's book, *The Marketing Imagination*, he talks about the "differentiation of anything." I love that phrase. It speaks directly to the fact that nothing is a commodity—or at least it shouldn't be! Levitt encourages marketers to think about their products in terms of concentric rings or circles that create almost a dartboard type of diagram. The circles represent the state of one's product, from the innermost ring, *generic* or commodity-like, to a middle circle of what's *expected* by the customer, all the way to the outermost circle that maximizes the *potential* of the product.

Think again of Levitt's generic circles in terms of the businesses we've discussed. This is the "nothing special" grocery store or the typical city parking garage—the basic of basics in any business. Now consider how these businesses (and maybe your business) can begin to grow out of each ring to advance to the next. This advancement is clearly what will differentiate your business and expose you to the full potential of your products and services. The outer circle is what takes you to the Service Star level.

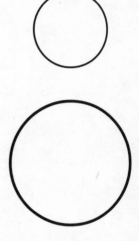

Inner circle examples:
standard business hours
an 800 number
validated parking
one-year warranty
traditional packaging

Outer circle examples:
personalized customer follow-up
Internet shopping
powerful guarantee or warranty
delivery versus pickup

The Outer Circle Experience

It's really about staying ahead. Each time you take a step upward (or advance to an outer ring), be prepared for a Chaser to step right into your footprint. But do not let this discourage you. Personally, I find that a review of outer circle service by others is the best inspiration to begin applying some creativity to your own activities. Following are just a few to stir your imagination.

Who Deserves the Credit	The Outer Circle Event
Hospital Women's Care Center	While many hospitals have gifts for new mothers when a baby is born, they don't have the impact of the gift given by this hospital in Jacksonville, Florida. They send their new families flowers one month after they've returned home from the hospital. You see, by this time the supporting family and friends have returned to their lives. The other flowers have died, and it's a time when reality often sets in. What better time to send a gift that says we're thinking of you!
Southeastern Utility	*Powerful* Guarantee. If your electric power is not turned on the day it was promised, you'll receive a $100 check for every day it's late. While this is not printed anywhere or offered at the time the service order is placed, it's an after-the-fact commitment that builds tremendous forgiveness for the error. In fact, most customers begin to say, "Hey, take your time!" A utility no less? Almost unbelievable.
Bank Teller	Having noticed that many folks have dogs with them as they come through the drive-in window at the bank, this teller took it upon herself to always keep a box of dog biscuits handy. Customers rave about this unexpected treat. What a personal statement of appreciation.
Dentist	This dentist simply listened to his patients continually mention their difficulty in breaking from work during the week. He decided to shift his hours to include evenings until eight. Imagine caring for the patients as well as their teeth.
Corporate Information System Troubleshooter	When her clients have a computer problem, she's the first one they call. Not only does she work diligently to correct the problem, but she makes a follow-up call the next day to ensure that all is going smoothly.
Amazon.com	Ever place an order with them? Before you have a chance to sign off the Internet, they've sent you a response that confirms receipt of your order, the price, the ship date, and of course a thank-you for your business—instant acknowledgment using technology to its fullest.
Hotel Desk Clerk	It's an everyday practice for this hotel to serve freshly baked cookies in their lobby from 5:00 to 7:00 P.M. When a tired traveler mentioned how much he appreciated them, three cookies and a note awaited him in his room the following evening. Wow, they know what makes this author tick!
Major 800# Call Center	Although the annoying recorded message greets you, this center is programmed to tell you the approximate wait time for your call to be answered. Now you can make the call on whether this suits your schedule. Should you need to call back, they even tell you the best times of the day to reach a representative quickly.

Someone Has Figured It Out

There is a bank in our community that is well known for its service to customers. They have truly distinguished themselves in service. This bank is hardly mentioned in a conversation without someone commenting on its service attributes in the first 60 seconds. In a conversation with the bank's president one day, he said, "You know, I hope all of my competitors stay around as long as my bank is around." Responding to the quizzical look on my face, he added, "You see, they sure make me look good. If I were the only game in town, people would not recognize how special my services are." Now here is someone who has figured it out. Your customers ARE your business and they notice when you do the unexpected.

Allow 15 minutes per exercise below.

Exercise

EXERCISE: SHOOTING FOR THE STARS

A. Working individually, each team member should take two minutes and list some activities or attributes of your team or organization that are Complacent. Now take another three minutes to list Doer activities or attributes for your team/organization.

Now as a group, take 10 minutes to have team members describe the items on their list. Specifically see if you can discuss how some Complacent items may be changed or enhanced in order to move them into the Doer box.

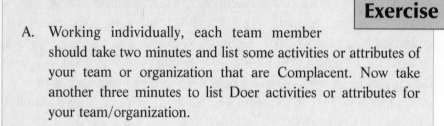

	Complacents			Doers	
1.	_____	→	1.	_____	
2.	_____	→	2.	_____	
3.	_____	→	3.	_____	
4.	_____	→	4.	_____	
5.	_____	→	5.	_____	

B. Working as a team, take 10 minutes and brainstorm opportunities/ideas that could move your organization into the Star box. Once you've listed the ideas, take five minutes and vote on the best ideas (we suggest no more than four or five ideas).

Service Star Ideas:

1. _____

_____

2. _____

_____

3. _____

4. _____

5. _____

Exercise

C. Finally, taking 15 minutes, expand on realistic ways in which the Service Star ideas can be implemented. Determine specific activities that need to happen, who will be the owner of the activities, and set a date when this activity should be accomplished.

	IDEA	WHAT NEEDS TO HAPPEN	WHO	WHEN
1.				
2.				
3.				
4.				

It's a Wrap

Did you catch all of the following points?

Plot your customer service program
- ★ You and your team
- ★ Your company
- ★ Your product or service lines
- ★ Your competitors

From Clueless to Stardom
- ★ Clueless—"The light's on but nobody's home"
- ★ Complacents—"Canahhepya?"
- ★ Chasers—"I will follow you anywhere"
- ★ Lightbulbs—"One day we should get around to . . ."
- ★ Doers—"What a great idea...let's start today!"
- ★ Stars—"Nobody does it better"

The inner circle is only average . . . move to the outer circle, please!

Mirror, Mirror:
A Self Assessment

Imagine a mirror, a very large mirror. In fact, it covers an entire wall, floor to ceiling, and it's at least 20 feet long. Now picture yourself standing in the middle of a room looking into this wall of glass. Of course you see yourself. There you are, head to toe, but we want you to look deeper. We want you to picture all of the support systems around you—all of the systems that affect the job that you do for your company or organization. And once you have a really good image, start making a list of all the support systems and people that you see in your mirror.

We'll help you get started. You should see computers, not only the hardware, but the software too. You see the people responsible for keeping them running. You see the lights, the phones, the policy manuals on the

shelf, and you see the people that make them work. You might see accounting and human resources folks, the sales staff, the engineers, and those responsible for making the products you sell. You may see delivery trucks and drivers, schedulers, trainers, and quality assurance inspectors. Somewhere in that reflection you see your supervisors, managers, owners, and/or shareholders. You spot the cleaning crew and facility maintenance workers. And if you look hard enough you'll see your family, friends, and significant others who may impact your life.

Now burn this image into your head and don't lose it. We ask you to do this because it's important that you realize your role in the organization and how dramatically you and the job that you do are affected by the actions and results of others.

A final request: Step through this imaginary mirror to the other side. On this side you will greet your customer. Whether it is by phone or face-to-face is unimportant. What is significant, however, is that you are not standing in front of a two-way mirror. This mirror, like most, is opaque on the backside. The customer cannot see all of the people behind you, they just see you! You are the reflection of the company.

Pointing Fingers

Weren't we all taught how rude this is? I can still hear my mother saying, "Do not point!" as I cast my finger directly at a man who had broken line for a ticket at the movie theater. But how else was I to make sure she knew who did this terrible wrong if I didn't point him out. Could I possibly describe him such that she could pick him out from the other 20 to 30 people in line? Did I expect her to go confront him and tell him of his wrongful ways? The fact is it didn't matter. You see, I was missing the point. Was the fact that he cut in line the issue? As much as it angered me, that wasn't the issue for my mother. Sure she didn't like me physically pointing, but the real issue was that I was blaming another for my situation, as if somehow that would make it better.

Now let's put that incident into the context of customer care. When was the last time you were being served and the representative with whom you were dealing cast blame elsewhere for your lack of being served? It happens all the time. Let's review a couple of instances, and for a few minutes put yourself in the place of the customer. What impressions do you walk away with?

EVENT ONE

You have decided to buy a new leaf blower. You go to a large hardware center in your area because you want selection, not to mention advice. You've located the lawn tools section, and, after a few minutes, you catch the attention of a salesman. This guy knows all there is to know about leaf blowers. He talks you into the battery powered because it's lighter to carry—easier to handle. You have a concern, however. Does it really have the power to blow leaves when they are damp or in shrubbery beds? "Of course," says the salesman, "they don't call it the little hurricane for nothing." You're sold and off you go with your new lawn toy.

It's now Saturday morning and you're trying out the "little hurricane." First disappointment and then frustration sets in. It seems your "little hurricane" is not much more than a hair dryer. You immediately return to the place of purchase to lodge your complaint and to upgrade your unit. And guess what you hear at the Customer Service Counter? "I don't know why the salespeople here keep telling people that these units have power. They don't. In fact, we must get two or three returned a week. Let me take care of this for you."

Now the customer care representative has been most helpful. Are you feeling any better about having selected this store? Unlikely. Are you feeling any better about this customer care representative? At least she's been honest. You see, you may be feeling that it's not her fault, she's not to blame, and how unfortunate it is that she gets to do the dirty deed of explaining the circumstances to you. Stop there. This is the key point. She has merely transferred any anger and frustration you may have to the salesman, the store, and even the product manufacturer. And yes, off of her. The bottom line is that you as a customer got the shaft.

EXERCISE

If you were the customer care representative, what are some things you could have said to keep the customer pleased with your store, the products, and your personal service?

Exercise

Things you could have said to the customer:

1. _____

2. _____

3. _____

4. _____

EVENT TWO

You're rushing home from work. You make a quick stop by the dry cleaners to pick up a suit for a special occasion that evening. You are rushed but feeling good about the night ahead. You get home, shower, and start to dress. It's 6:30 P.M. You're OK, but with no time to spare. As you dress you notice something is not right with your suit. The collar on the front left side has something that appears to be a grease smudge on it. You feel your entire mood starting to change. Why now? Why me? Is this an omen for the night ahead? The fact is you have no choice. You change quickly but not without thinking an unkind word or two about the dry cleaners.

On the way to work the next morning you stop by the cleaners to show them the suit. Do you think they showed the empathy you were wanting? Not likely. Instead, the man behind the counter said, "That's the third item returned this morning with this same kind of mark on it." He goes on to explain how the suit is pressed, giving very specific information on just how the grease may have gotten there. While you may have appreciated the lesson in Dry Cleaning 101, it hasn't done anything to solve your problem. It was yet another finger-pointing that did nothing to make you feel any better about this particular dry cleaners. Don't you wonder who checks the clothes before they are bagged and hung for the customers? How old is the pressing equipment? What if the stain doesn't come out? What are they going to do about it?

Exercise

EXERCISE
Make a list of things that the dry cleaner could have said that you would like to have heard. Now, assume the suit doesn't come clean. List two actions that you would expect to keep you a loyal customer.

Things the dry cleaner could have said:

1. _____
2. _____
3. _____
4. _____

Actions to keep you a loyal customer:
1. _____
2. _____
3. _____
4. _____

If there is one very important lesson to take away from this chapter it's that while people can be at fault, it's far more critical to understand the *systems* behind those people. For example, did the hardware center or the dry cleaner have a plan in place to offer something to the customer for their inconvenience, cost, and aggravation? Did the dry cleaner have a maintenance schedule for the equipment? Was it, in fact, someone's job to check the apparel before it went to the customer? We could build a long list. The fact is that over 90 percent of the problems in organizations are the fault of systems, not people. Thinking proactively, we must then ask ourselves what system could prevent this problem from occurring again. And if a system is in place, then what performance review mechanism is in place for addressing it with the employee who failed to follow the procedure? Almost any way you look at it, the first action following a service breakdown should be a review of the system, not the fixing of blame on an associate.

Don't forget, however, your job as the frontline associate is to be prepared with the *right words* to cover for a bad system. One of the best examples of this is when computers are down in a call center. Don't you get tired of hearing, "I can't check your records right now because our system is down." What a negative. How about, "Let me make a note of that. Our system is updating now, but I will make that change and call you back if I have any questions at that time." Notice the difference?

Rewards Work, Just Ask My Dog

Once you've looked at your systems and processes and determined that they are solid, it is time to look at the people part of the equation. And as we all know, one of the most important components of the "people factor" is recognition and reward.

I happen to love dogs. I also love a book by the famous dog trainer, Barbara Woodhouse. Her book, *No Bad Dogs*, says it all—"There's no such thing as a bad dog, just a bad owner." What she's conveying, of course, is that response follows reward. Aren't people the same? People repeat the behavior that's rewarded. It works that easily. I'm not for a moment saying that we're all dogs, it's just basic nature and an instinct that we share.

Ever wonder why so many managers are stingy with praise? I find that too often we are asked to do things, we do them, and yet we don't hear thanks for a job well done. It's not that managers are truly bad people who don't appreciate the work. It's just that they are busy, focused on the next task, and, most likely, they were never trained in the art of appreciation. Just like outstanding customer service, this is a behavior that needs training and cultivation.

Rewards and recognition can be fun to structure. I know one group at the Department of Defense that instituted a "Mistake of the Month Award." If you catch a mistake and fix it you get a firefighter's hat as an award—a symbol that says you put out the fire. When the fire hat transfers, you get a small baby hat to set on your desk or computer. Some people have six or seven lined up. They love these fire hats because it shows that they went above and beyond. If you would like some really neat stuff on recognition and reward ideas, read Bob Nelson's book, *1001 Ways to Reward Employees*.

Recognition Tips

- ★ Be specific. Thank people for something in particular such as, "I really liked the way you helped that elderly gentleman who was lost. You showed such care and compassion."
- ★ Don't underestimate the value of small rewards. A handshake, note, or kind words can mean so much.
- ★ Be timely. To point out a situation of praise at the six-month evaluation just loses its punch.
- ★ Be sincere. I don't think this warrants any more comment.
- ★ When appropriate, make the recognition public and make it fun.

Note to team members: Recognition is not sacred ground for team leaders and other management. Think of how well it works to recognize and reward peers and other teams that you work with. Pick a team member that you can recognize in the next 12 hours and use the tips above!

Another company noted for its recognition programs is Southwest Airlines. The company's president, Herb Kelleher, is a very colorful individual. You've doubtless heard about some of his antics to create enthusiasm. He's dressed up as Elvis while helping to deal with baggage issues. He shows up regularly at team meetings. He runs numerous contests, and his attitude and sense of service are unmistakable. Try flying them sometime. Employees are enthusiastic; they have fun; they make crazy announcements. Just call their 800 number and you are likely to hear one of them.

Back to Our Mirror

For the remainder of this chapter we will walk you (and/or your customer care team) through an assessment of your organization's support systems. Our focus will be specifically on those aspects that pertain to delivering exceptional customer care.

Allow 15 minutes to complete the following tables.

Exercise

EXERCISE: MAPPING THE GAPS I

Mapping the Gaps is a straightforward way to assess where you are versus where you believe you should be. For each area you are asked to rank the performance of your company to the statements provided. Remember, we are not pointing fingers but diagnosing system failures or *gaps* in your customer care program. The following rankings should be used (insert NA if not applicable):

You Must Be Joking	Maybe on a Good Day	Proud to Say That's Us
1—3	4—7	8—10

Let's start at the beginning point:

THE HIRING PROCESS

Support System for Delivering Exceptional Customer Care	Rank (1-10)
Part of our organization's interview process directly assesses customer care skills.	
We only hire people with proven customer care experience.	
We role-play candidates in challenging customer situations.	
We provide candidates with our organization's expectations for service.	
Our orientation process includes specific emphasis on customer care.	Avg. Score
TOTAL SCORE	

TRAINING

Support System for Delivering Exceptional Customer Care	Rank (1-10)
We have specific training that is required for all personnel involved with direct customer contact.	
We have refresher training courses on customer care at least annually.	
Each new customer care associate has an experienced mentor or buddy to whom he or she is assigned.	
Our new customer care associates monitor live customer interactions for an adequate period of time before being asked to handle them independently.	
Following the training, our performance is evaluated before we begin working with customers.	Avg. Score
TOTAL SCORE	

PERFORMANCE REVIEW, RECOGNITION, AND REWARD

Support System for Delivering Exceptional Customer Care	Rank (1-10)
Our associates have periodic reviews made of their customer care performance.	
Feedback on performance is given in a timely and constructive way.	
Training is directly tied to the areas identified for performance improvement.	
We have an effective recognition system which highlights exceptional performance.	
Outstanding customer care delivery is rewarded in our organization.	
Our management understands the importance of exceptional customer care.	Avg. Score
TOTAL SCORE	

POLICIES & PROCEDURES

Support System for Delivering Exceptional Customer Care	Rank (1-10)	
Customers can access us 24 hours a day, 6 or 7 days a week.		
We have strong guarantees that stand behind our products and/or services.		
Our customer care associates have a reasonable "spending authority" to do what is right for the customer.		
If we disappoint a customer, we have contingency plans to help make up for the bad experience.		
Our organization conducts a Customer Satisfaction Survey at least annually.		
We track customers who have stopped doing business with us.		
We contact "lost customers" to find out why they stopped doing business with us.		
We conduct an Employee Satisfaction Survey at least once a year.		
Associates are encouraged to submit suggestions for improved service.		
Our company believes in solving the customer problem "on the spot" as opposed to referring it to another department or "up the line" of management.		Avg. Score
TOTAL SCORE		

TECHNOLOGY

Support System for Delivering Exceptional Customer Care	Rank (1-10)	
Our phone system is customer-friendly.		
Our customers' first interaction with our organization is warm and inviting.		
We don't have to ask for the same customer information repeatedly when dealing with different areas of our company.		
Our information systems are up-to-date and user friendly.		
We use technology wisely to enhance, not detract from, a customer's experience.		
Customers can interact with our company via the Internet.		Avg. Score
TOTAL SCORE		

OTHER SUPPORT OPERATIONS

Support System for Delivering Exceptional Customer Care	Rank (1-10)	
Our products/services are delivered in a timely manner.		
Our advertising accurately reflects the way we do business.		
Our physical facilities are inviting to the customer inside and out.		
Signage in our facilities is pleasant and helps direct the customer.		
Our products/services are a good value to the customer.		
Our billing/invoicing is accurate and easy to read.		
We thank the customer for their business in sincere and creative ways.		Avg. Score
TOTAL SCORE		

Exercise

EXERCISE: MAPPING THE GAPS II

So how did you do? In order to evaluate yourself fairly, do the following:

1. Total your score by category.
2. If you are doing this exercise as part of a team, first calculate an average score for the team, per statement, across all tables.
3. Take the total for each section and divide by the number of statements to determine your average score per category.
4. Select your five lowest ranking statements across all categories and highlight them.

Having completed these tables, you might be having any number of feelings. You could be sitting a little straighter in your chair—proud of your organization. This is unlikely. Customer care is still in such need of improvement in most businesses. If you are where most are, you may be feeling a little overwhelmed, possibly discouraged, about how your organization is ranking. It is important that you flip that attitude to one of enthusiasm for the opportunities you have to improve. Easy to say, but not always easy to do.

It is not easy to guide you from this assessment to implementation. Each organization is different. Implementing corrective action to some of the issues outlined in your exercise may be completely within your control. Other issues may need assistance or approval by others. In the latter case, your documentation should be very helpful in making a case for system improvement.

Allow 15 minutes to complete the following analysis.

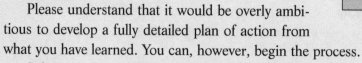

EXERCISE: MAPPING THE GAPS III
Building a Service Plan

Exercise

Please understand that it would be overly ambitious to develop a fully detailed plan of action from what you have learned. You can, however, begin the process.

Select your two lowest (average score) categories from the six evaluated. Write the category in the space below and then list a minimum of three U-turn activities or ideas that would address the desired outcome.

Support System:

1. _____
2. _____
3. _____

Support System:

1. _____
2. _____
3. _____

Note to team leaders and team members: Whatever you do, don't stop here. Take these exercises and ideas back to your team and/or your team leader. Let them give input to the process as well. It is recommended that you involve at least five to seven others in the process.

Have these folks come up with their own U-turn ideas. Then, as a group, discuss these ideas. Now do three things:

1. Establish priorities for attention.
2. Assign an individual responsible for plan development and implementation.
3. Determine timetable, measurements for success, and progress report intervals.

It's a Wrap

Did you catch all of the following points?

The service mirror has two faces

★ Reflections—you and your support systems

★ The mirror image—your customer sees only you

Don't pass the blame . . . fix the problem

★ Customer doesn't care who, just what

★ Over 90 percent of problems are systems, not people

★ Your job: find the right words to cover for a bad system

Pavlov's people

★ Rewards and recognition work . . . and not just for your pet!

★ Tips: timely, sincere, specific, fun!

CHAPTER FIVE

Let's Talk about Me: Things You Can Do!

It's one of those days. The alarm clock just went off and the last thing you want to do is get out of bed. You can't believe it's time. Whoa. You look out the window and see what a rotten day it is. And you say, "I can't believe I've got to get out in that stuff!" But you finally get up, and you go in the bathroom to look in the mirror. What happens to us overnight anyway? I mean, rarely do you say, "Whew! Sure am looking good this morning!" And then you head off to the kitchen to eat one of those fiber cereals. I don't know if you've noticed, but it seems the more you chew that fiber bran stuff, it just grows in your mouth. Then you finally get in your car, and, naturally, you're behind the slowest car. Do you know this feeling? And you still have a full day of work to face

BULLSEYE

with lots of demanding customers. How do you leave behind that kind of start to your day?

How do we keep ourselves up and going all day long? How do we keep that positive attitude? How can we possibly deliver exceptional customer care without that positive attitude? It's not easy. You have a job that is, day-in and day-out, never giving you a chance to regroup. You fill a lot of roles in your job. Think about what customers expect. They expect you to be part detective, part teacher, part negotiator, part financial consultant, and often amateur therapist. It's expected that you are to be nice, pleasant, interested, concerned, empathetic—and all for eight hours a day. Isn't this where you go home at night and the last thing you want to be is nice? You justify, "I've done that already, so leave me be!" The fact is, this is our role. Serving customers comes with a great deal of pressure and stress. This is why the frontline is often times called the "firing line."

The Wrong Side of the Bed

With all of the expectations that customers have of us, it's amazing we can even climb out of bed. We tell ourselves it's going to be a rotten day and, guess what, the day becomes that. We almost look for things that are rotten in the day. Admit it, don't you know people who do this, people who do it almost every day? They are negative people. You know the type. You walk in and say, "Good morning," and they snap back, "What's so good about it?" Here's the scary thing, and it's what learning experts are telling us. These experts tell us that 80 percent of our internal dialogue is negative. Ouch, 80 percent! The majority of things that we talk to ourselves about are negative.

Self-Talk

Talking to ourselves is normal. At least *silently* talking to ourselves is normal. If you talk out loud, and many of us do, be careful—they may lock you up. One of the things to help you is not less talking but less negative talking. Your self-talk can make or break how you feel about yourself, how you feel about your day, how you feel about the customer you are about to handle. I'm not here to say that positive thinking always works, but I do say negative thinking almost never works!

Note to team members: You can learn much more about the effects of positive thinking in a book by Maxwell Maltz, M.D., FICS, Psycho-Cybernetics. *Also check out* What to Say When You Talk to Yourself *by Shad Helmstetter, Ph.D.*

Learn to listen to your self-talk. If you hear a lot of negatives, change your self-talk to support you. Don't set yourself up to have it work against you. Think about the things we sometimes say to ourselves when beginning to deal with a customer. Be honest with yourself. We say things like: "I can't believe she goes out in public looking like that." or "Listen to that accent." Face it, we humans have biases, and these biases (sometimes prejudices) affect the way we posture ourselves in our servicing. When these negatives creep in, we fail to be as professional as we could be. So stop the creep.

There are a number of ways to keep your attitude up. Look for all the positives you can in a situation. Let's say, for sake of discussion, you are a bank teller. It's Friday, it's payday, and the lines are backed up. You typically tell yourself, "I don't think I can take one more customer. Will this line ever end?" The truth is, in interviewing tellers, that what they say makes for really awful days is slow business. It makes for a boring day. And the days that the customers are not in the bank are inevitably the days that the tellers are out of balance at their window. Funny, isn't it. The busy days are the ones that they always balance. In recognizing this, the tellers can begin to self-talk themselves into appreciating the customer-upon-customer day.

A great example of self-talk came from a Hallmark Halloween card someone sent me. On the card there are two jack-o'-lanterns. One has been carved with a frowning face. The other has a smiling face. The frowning pumpkin says, "I hate this stinking holiday. I could be back in the pumpkin patch, sucking up a few herbicides through my vine, but no!

I gotta sit here with a candle in my guts, waiting for my head to cave in." The smiling pumpkin then says, "Wow, Halloween is really neat. Look at all those cute kids. They seem so happy! Hey, my head is caving in! Boy, oh boy, is this fun!" I think of these jack-o'-lanterns often. The card goes on to say, "The face you carve has a tremendous psychological effect on your jack-o'-lantern. So carve responsibly. Carve with care. And this year, carve happy." What are you carving everyday?

If I Were the Betting Type

There's an old concept called the 90/10 rule. Ninety percent of the things that happen to us are decent; 10 percent aren't; and we focus on the 10 percent. A good example of this is our media—especially the news media. Most tend to focus on the 10 percent that are bad to the point that we start to think the whole world is coming apart at the seams.

Now, think of your customers. The same statistic holds true for them. Ninety percent of them are good, decent folks. Ten percent go against the grain. Somehow, for some reason, we focus on that 10 percent. So I want you to take a bet. Start focusing on the 90 percent that are good and see if it doesn't make a difference in your life. I know it does. It works for me, and I've been told countless times how it has worked for others. Take the odds—go with the 90.

Tip for the Day

Don't we all know a negative person? You say, "Good morning," and they reply, "What's so good about it?" Their day is programmed to be negative, and it can influence you. Be careful of how you let others affect your attitude, and, more importantly, try to use your own positive influence to help those around you that need it.

The Great Escape

Looking at things more positively and using powerful self-talk can be great strategies for keeping your attitude up. But let's be real. There are certain times (or with certain customers) that you need more options for keeping a smile on your face. One option that is often taken for granted is to use your breaks wisely. I am disheartened whenever I observe someone who chooses to take a break to vent (gripe is a better word) about everything that's just gone wrong in his day. While one could argue that this type of venting can be therapeutic; most often it just causes one to relive an irritating moment. Before you know it, he's almost as angry as when the incident took place originally. Don't get caught in this trap, and do what you can to get your team members out of this mode as well. It's helpful to get away from the stress of intense customer contact. Try going for a walk, reading something enjoyable, listening to music, or maybe an inspirational tape.

Break Wisely

★ Take a walk.

★ Read a magazine or book.

★ Listen to relaxing or uplifting music.

★ Eat a snack (chocolate or fruit—it's your conscience).

★ Take time for a hobby (from crosswords to cross-stitch).

★ Play cards or a board game.

★ Write a letter to a friend, family member, or even someone in your organization whom you admire.

★ Start your holiday gift list (it's never too early).

And for those many hours when you are at your desk, be sure you have something there that evokes good feelings. These are called *anchors*. Anchors might include a photo, a vacation spot cut from a magazine, or fresh flowers. The reason they are called anchors is that they help anchor you to a place where you feel good. Many people pin funny cartoons around, and these are wonderful releases for the workday. For me, one of my anchors is my dog. If you are a pet owner, you understand this. I have this wonderful picture of my dog in mid-sneeze. It's a hilarious picture. You can't see it without making comment. It's a great anchor.

Attitude Anchors

★ Photos of loved ones

★ Cards, usually humorous

★ Cartoons

★ Scripture or poem

★ Motivational quote

★ Letter of praise

★ Plant or fresh flowers

★ Candy dish

★ Vacation pictures

★ Artwork

Notes

Note to team member: Need more help? Place a check beside the anchors or break ideas that you want to try. Also, see if you and your team can add to this list. Act on this before the week ends.

Another way to keep the attitude up is to simply take care of yourself. Watch what you eat, exercise, and take up a good hobby. These things have long been proven to help reduce the stress and burnout of our jobs. Don't dismiss them lightly.

And finally, bring your sense of humor with you wherever you go. One organization I know of has formalized this habit by creating a humor break. The break includes a cart of fun from which party type items are dispensed—hats, kazoos, balloons. This may sound silly, but it works wonders. The responsibility for the humor break rotates weekly, and you never know what to expect. It's fun, it gives people a chance to relax, and it reinforces energy and attitude. Similarly, an environmental laboratory started a program called Save Our Sanity (SOS). It began during very busy times when employees were being asked to work unusual amounts of overtime. The company recognized that work demands were intense, so they began having a cart of goodies pass through the company several afternoons a week. The cart was filled with fruits, cookies, and candy bars. It was not only a sign that the company cared and recognized the efforts being put forth, but it provided a little lift in the day for the workers.

You Versus Your Role

In your role as a customer care associate, you are the embodiment of your organization. Remember standing on the backside of the mirror in Chapter 4? All the customer sees is you. We know this, yet sometimes we let down our guard. Often this is where service, as perceived by the customer, begins to slip and fail.

Recently I was sitting on an airplane. Unlike most flights, I was able to get a first class seat due to my frequent flier program and seat availability. So I'm sitting there contently, waiting for the flight to depart. Next, a flight attendant breezes through the curtain from coach, approaches the cockpit, and instructs the pilot, "We need some air on back here. The sardines are starting to cook." Isn't that a revealing comment? So that's how the airlines think of us—their customers. We are paying, quite handsomely, I might add, to be on this flight, and to them we are nothing more than sardines in a box. I assure you we began to feel that way. What indifference this flight attendant showed to her customers. Some might say she was rude. In either case she allowed her role to slip away. Surely she wouldn't have said what she did in earshot of the coach passengers, and did she really think it was acceptable for those in front of the curtain? Let's hope not.

This type of slippage is damaging. More often than not it takes place when one employee is talking with another, and there's a customer there too. The conversation wasn't intended for the customers' ears, but they heard. I can't count the number of conversations regarding work schedules that I've personally overheard. You've heard them. You're standing at a counter and one employee says to the other, "I'm going on break now," or "see you Saturday, I'm starting weekend shifts." Does this really warrant discussion in front of the customer?

The Disney Institute at Walt Disney World has a wonderful program for curbing this type of inappropriate behavior. At Disney World, they don't have employees; they have cast members. And as a cast member you have a role. Whether your job is within an attraction, on stage, or behind a cash register, you clearly have a role in the Disney experience. They call it *onstage* and *offstage*. What a simple and clear concept.

When you are within the theme park grounds, you are there for the customer and you are onstage. And during that time you would no more break from your role than you would in delivering a script on stage. It's part of what makes the Disney experience so special.

The key to making the onstage/offstage concept work is the offstage dimension. We've talked about the pressure and stress that come with the customer care role. It is not realistic to think that someone could stay "in role" 100 percent of the time. We can't. So for these times we need a place to escape, to get out of eyeshot and earshot of the customer. A friend relayed an experience to me recently in which he witnessed a rather ugly employee confrontation at the counter of a fast food restaurant. Apparently the manager had asked an employee to open a register to help with the lines. The employee snapped back with, "Make up your mind, you just told me to go clean up the tables." You can imagine the discussion that followed. The ordeal ended with the manager asking the employee to leave; the employee threw down her cap and marched out to her car. How awkward for the 10 or so people standing in line. How awkward for the other employees.

Remember the importance of staying in your role. Serving customers is demanding. Keep in mind that you have many options available to help you create the customer experience. Be creative and use good judgement. You and your customers will be happier for it.

Taking Ownership

No matter what industry you work in, or what company you work for, there will be problems. Some are caused by the company, some by the customer, some by acts of God, and some by you. It's one of those darn facts of life. And as trite as the phrase can be, I've always loved the message, *it's not the cards you're dealt, it's how you play them that counts*. This same philosophy of living has been packaged in numerous creative ways: 100 Percent Responsibility, Own the Problem, Act Like an Owner. You've heard more, I'm sure. Like so many trite phrases, we know them but we don't live them. And why not? The improvements we would all see by living them would be astounding.

I heard a counselor speak recently to a group of employees, and he talked about his years as a marriage counselor. One of the first things he would ask his couples is, "So how does your marriage work? Give it to me in percentages. Is it 75/25, 50/50? Each of you write it down and don't confer. Just be honest." Invariably people would come back with some split that gave him a good indication of his work ahead.

In all of his years he never once had an individual give him what he professed to be the right answer. The right answer (or the goal to strive for anyway) is 100/100. You see if each individual in a marriage would treat all situations as if he or she were 100 percent responsible, then most of your time would be spent thanking the other for taking care of things that you really felt *you* should have done. What a concept! Just imagine: "Those aren't my dishes in the sink, but I'll clean them up anyway." "The lawn is getting a little shaggy, I better mow it." "The dog needs a bath, come on Fido!"

The key here is both partners are giving 100 percent. What if one partner starts this concept and the other continues to loaf? Don't you think after a while a little resentment would build? "OK, I've been doing this 100 percent junk for three weeks now, and I don't see you chipping in. In fact, I think you see it as a little bit of a free ride." Simply put, that's not 100 percent ownership, that's keeping score. And keeping score is one of the most destructive tactics one can apply. To truly embrace 100 percent, you adopt it with no questions asked, no scorecard kept, no trial period established. You see it's a way of life. It's deciding that you can control the situation before you, and you are the one to make it right. Is this simplistic? Yes. You can come up with thousands of "yeh, but's." Can you do everything? No. Can you be taken advantage of? Yes. More importantly, however, does this philosophy provide for better outcomes and a happier existence than blaming others? Yes, yes, yes!

Now take this 100 percent ownership philosophy into your work experience and, most specifically, the customer care context. Pretend you are a bank teller again. A customer just walked in and said her ATM card was eaten in the machine. You could:

a. tell her that she needs to fill out a new application and mail it into the customer care center three states away;

b. tell her to go to the other side of the bank and wait for the next available personal banker;

c. tell her she probably will save some money by not having an ATM card anyway; or

d. after showing appropriate empathy for her loss, pick up the phone, or complete the application on her behalf. You also let her know not only when to expect a new ATM card, but what options she has in the interim.

Why is it that the last choice is selected so rarely in real life? After all, it's not my job! If we all took a vote on the most irritating phrases in the human language, "It's not my job" has to rank in the top five. It's right in there with, "That's not what you ordered," and "I told you so."

To the benefit of the employees—those of us trying to do right by the customer—two real things do stand in our way. First, most companies aren't structured for 100 percent ownership. By this I mean if you spent time making sure that each and every customer was helped to the best of your ability, would you be getting done the specific items covered in your job description? You might not handle the expected volume of contacts or calls. Furthermore, there is someone being paid by the company to do just this task, so why should you? Secondly, you may not have had the proper training to perform certain tasks. These boundaries have merit, but there is still ground that can be paved. For example, don't bother with the fact that you can't help the customer. Instead, explain who can help them and provide the proper introduction. From a customer's perspective, think of the difference in being redirected or passed off versus being personally introduced with a recap of your needs to the person that can provide the help you need. By doing this you are taking ownership.

This is a small example, but when I was lost in one of those major home building/lumber-to-go type places and asked for help to find caulking, I was flippantly told, "Try aisle 12." Well, the "try" didn't make me feel altogether comfortable, and guess what, aisle 12 was hinges and springs for doors. Had the representative either walked with me to aisle 12, looked in a computer, or (can you imagine) offered to go get the item for me, maybe I would not have felt like I was in this huge, impersonal, warehouse of a building.

A Few Ways You Can Take Ownership

1. How are you handling the caller who's been transferred twice already?
2. Do you actively look for people who appear lost or in need of assistance?
3. Are you detecting an uncertainty in a customer's voice that indicates he or she doesn't fully understand?
4. When you are busy, do you acknowledge the presence of a customer who is waiting and let him or her know when someone will be available?
5. Do you follow up with a customer to make sure that his or her needs were met, even if by another team member?

Taking ownership is really about leaving the customer in a better condition than when the contact was first established. If the customer was frustrated, did you help calm him down and provide a solution? If she was simply transacting basic business, did you do something extra to build a relationship with her? The following exercise is a simple way to build awareness of the service quality of your customer contacts.

Exercise

The time needed to complete this exercise is minimal; however, you should do this chart for 10 to 20 contacts a day for at least two weeks.

EXERCISE: CHARTING L'ATTITUDES

Use the table below or create your own such that you can carry it with you. The table should be easy to access throughout your day. After each customer contact, both face-to-face and over the telephone, put a tally stroke in the row that best applies to the attitude of the customer at the beginning and end of your contact. Use the following legend as a guide for the customer's attitude:

+customer very satisfied and happy
=customer OK, problem resolved
− customer was not satisfied and/or frustrated

BEGIN	END	TALLY OF CUSTOMERS
+	+	
+	=	
+	−	
=	+	
=	=	
=	−	
−	+	
−	=	
−	−	

By completing this table daily, you will begin to change your behavior. At first you will notice the effort it takes to put a positive spin on each and every contact. Before long it will become second nature. You should find that this exercise also helps you recognize the 90 percent good versus the 10 percent not so good. At your team meetings, compare tables with one another. Talk about trends, highlights, and barriers. This chart should send you and your team members a message. What is it telling you?

It's a Wrap

Did you catch all of the following points?

The frontline is the "firing line"
★ Stress and pressures of dealing with customers
★ How do you keep a positive attitude all day?

Talk to yourself—but try not to answer!
★ Self-talk is normal and healthy
★ Try and keep it positive . . . watch out for negative creep
★ Remember the 90/10 rule: focus on the 90 percent of customers who are great

You deserve a break today
★ Get "offstage" for awhile
★ Read, walk, snack, listen to music
★ Keep an attitude anchor at your desk

Positive attitudes show (and so do negative ones)

One hundred percent ownership
★ "It's not my job" doesn't cut the mustard
★ Leave the customer in better shape than you found him or her

Hello and Goodbye:
First and Last Impressions

First Impressions

Business was kind of slow one very cold and rainy winter day at a luxury car dealership in Atlanta. Inside the showroom, the sales representatives were kicked back. It was just one of those dreary days when no one was particularly anxious to venture out on the lot and show cars. Around mid-morning the silence in the showroom was shattered by the loud sputtering of an old, muddy pickup truck pulling into the dealership. The truck stopped and out stepped a man who began walking around the lot. Probably just a "tire-kicker" out killing time, the sales team figured. After a few minutes, however, it became obvious this guy wasn't just going to look around for a couple of minutes then leave. He was seriously interested in

BULLSEYE

looking at new automobiles. "Who's up?" someone on the sales floor asked. "I'll pass," said one of the salesmen. "Not me," said a second. Finally, Bobby decided he would venture out and help the man in the pickup truck. You've probably figured out the story by now. The customer, we'll call him Joe, had his luxury car stolen from a convenience store parking lot a few weeks ago. All he had left to drive was his old hunting truck, and he was on a mission. After about 30 minutes, Bobby returned to the showroom with an unmistakable grin of satisfaction frozen (literally) on his face. It seems that Joe, the owner of a carpet mill, had just received his insurance settlement and proceeded to shell out $60,000 cash for a brand new automobile to replace his stolen one.

What's the moral of this true story? Be careful about forming impressions of your customers. You might be talking with Joe.

This chapter is about impressions, or perceptions as we sometimes call them. In the automobile story we just related, the service providers formed a negative perception of the customer (this is a country hick who couldn't possibly be in the market for a new luxury car), and as a result no one was in a hurry to serve.

Your customers also form impressions very quickly about you and your business. Former Scandinavian Airlines President Jan Carlzon coined the phrase "moments of truth" to describe these first impressions. According to Carlzon, a moment of truth occurs any time a customer comes in contact with your organization and has a chance to form an impression. It might be an ad, a business card, Web site home page, or telephone answering technique (we'll talk about automated telephone attendants later in the Technology chapter). Research reveals that we, as customers, form dozens of impressions about a business within the first few minutes of our service experience. Your challenge is to make these very positive moments of truth.

Here's a great story about positive moments of truth. Most of you have visited Walt Disney World in Orlando, Florida. The Disney organization does a lot of things extremely well in the area of customer service and is benchmarked regularly by organizations worldwide seeking to improve service levels. The Disney folks did some research a few years ago to determine the profile of their "average" visitor. The research showed that their visitors who traveled by automobile drove, on average, about eight hours from home to the park. The typical visiting family size was four. Now picture a hot day in the middle of the summer. Mom, dad, and two kids are locked in the minivan for eight hours together with the refrain "Are we almost there?" echoing constantly throughout the vehicle. Upon arrival in the Disney parking lot after this long day of driving (because the kids want to get right to the fun now and not wait until the next morning), Disney discovered that with great frequency, dads (or moms) were locking the keys inside their cars in their haste to get the kids out and running. Being the customer-oriented organization it is, Disney World doesn't want visitors unhappy even before they walk through the gates. So they hired a crew of professional locksmiths whose sole job is to drive through the parking lots (there are a lot of them!) looking for visitors in distress and unlocking their cars—free of charge! What a positive moment of truth! Instead of inner rage at such a careless act, and thus a negative feeling at the start of their visit (or end of the day if they don't immediately realize what they've done), those Disney World visitors now have a very positive image of the organization and are likely to feel that it can do no wrong! And as a benefit to Disney, the visitors will tell dozens of friends about their positive experience.

Maybe you've never locked your keys in the car at Disney World. Think of other experiences where you have formed first and lasting impressions. Have you ever gone into a restaurant and been seated, only to notice cracker crumbs on the floor, stains on the tablecloth, or dirty or unclean eating utensils? What perception do you now have of the cleanliness of the kitchen? Unfortunately, a negative one no doubt. You now start expecting bad food, bad service, and you'll probably find it (or at least what you now think is bad).

At 30,000 Feet It's Too Late

One of my favorite examples of negative perceptions comes from Tom Peters, author of a number of books including *The Wow Project*. Peters relates the story of an airline executive who said that when a passenger sits in his seat, pulls down his tray table, and sees coffee stains, he also sees poor engine maintenance. Professor Vincent Omochanu of the University of Miami, a noted expert on customer service, adds a bit to the analogy. When he travels, upon boarding his flight he first glances into the cockpit to quickly inspect the appearance of the pilot and copilot. As he proceeds to his seat, he makes the same observation of the flight attendants. Next he inspects around and under his seat for cleanliness and proof that the airplane was serviced. If these quick visual inspections are not to Professor Omochanu's liking, he wonders to himself whether the same policies that dictate grooming and cleanliness standards apply also to aircraft maintenance! He forms a negative perception of the entire airline based on observations of certain aspects of the operation. Do coffee stains or poorly groomed airline staff mean that aircraft maintenance is substandard? Who knows? It's the perception that matters. The question is, then, what are your organization's coffee stains? You will have a chance to answer that question later in this chapter.

Perceptions can also be positive. Ever take your dirty car in to be repaired and picked it up spotlessly clean? Many automobile repair shops routinely include a car wash as part of the service. For all you know, the place could only be washing cars, but because they took care of the outside, they must have taken care of the inside! That's a positive perception. If I take a shirt into my dry cleaners with a chipped or missing button, the shirt comes back not only freshly starched but with a replacement button—another positive moment of truth (especially the first time it happens).

Let's do an exercise on moments of truth. First read the example that follows of moments of truth developed for a local motor vehicles office. Next, work individually or with your team for a few minutes and list as many moments of truth as you can think of for your own organization. Remember, a moment of truth is any opportunity that a customer has to form a positive or negative impression of your organization. Be honest, and in this exercise don't concentrate so much on how you rate in each area but rather the moment of truth itself.

MOMENTS OF TRUTH
Department of Motor Vehicles
Anywhere, USA

Exercise

1. Toll-free information number
2. Availability of forms (and pencils) in the office
3. Length of lines (see note 1)
4. Queuing method used
5. Signage in the office
6. Attitude and knowledge of DMV staff
7. User friendliness (for example, is a large sign posted listing the paperwork requirements or do you find out what documents you are missing only after standing in line for an hour?)
8. Availability of parking
9. Accommodation for the elderly or handicapped
10. Hours of operation
11. Adequacy of staffing, especially during peak periods

Note 1: You might think that the DMV has no control over length of lines. In South Carolina, a DMV employee team suggested several measures, since adopted, to reduce lines. Among them were two-year registrations and registration by mail (you mail in your property tax to the county and they forward the receipt to the DMV, which then mails your tags to you). The goal: keep people from having to visit the DMV field office.

MOMENTS OF TRUTH
Your Organization

1. _____
2. _____
3. _____
4. _____
5. _____

Great Expectations

Let's take a closer look at how perceptions are formed, and let's start with expectations. As customers, we expect certain things with regard to product and service quality. We form these expectations based on a number of factors. It may be helpful to think of them as the CARE factors:

C ompetition
A dvertising
R eputation
E xperience

★ **Competition**—If one car dealership in the area offers weekend repair service, if one airline cuts its fares, or if a maker of personal computers or digital cameras drops its prices, we expect that others will follow suit (and usually they do!).

★ **Advertising**—Television, magazines and newspapers, the Internet—hundreds of millions of dollars are spent each year to promote products and services, building our expectations for a healthier, more comfortable lifestyle; finding the ultimate bargain, and on and on.

★ **Reputation**—Good old word of mouth is probably the strongest basis on which customers form expectations. "Do you know a good restaurant in the area?" "Who's the best Internet service provider?" "Who do you use to cut your hair?" These and other questions are asked and answered around the world millions of times each day. Not only do we give our recommendations on where to go (and not go) for goods and services, we use descriptions based on our most recent experience, which go a long way towards establishing the expectations of the listener. "The food is great at ABC Bistro, but the service could be better."

★ **Experience**—This applies to your product, service, or organization. If you've dealt with a business in the past, you've no doubt come to expect some level (high or low) of product quality and customer service.

Once expectations are established in the minds of customers (even before walking in the front door), the power of perception truly comes into play. I expect x (in terms of service quality). If I receive (or perceive) x plus 1, 2, 3, my expectations are exceeded and I feel that I have received exceptional customer service. On the other hand, if I receive (or perceive) x minus 1, 2, 3, a gap exists—and in that gap lies customer disappointment. It's a pretty simple formula. The problem is we may think we are doing all the right things and exceeding customer expectations, but unless we view our service delivery through the eyes and ears of those customers, we may well be coming up short.

We mentioned the American Customer Satisfaction Index earlier. Through a joint venture of the University of Michigan and the American Society for Quality, a national index was developed to measure, for the first time, customer satisfaction with goods and services in America. The American Customer Satisfaction Index utilizes sophisticated telephone sampling techniques to gauge consumer attitudes toward the quality of goods and services across a broad range of industry and government segments. One critical component of the survey instrument is a comparison between what customers expected prior to making a purchase (in terms of product quality and customer service), and their perception of the actual experience.

Here are two quick examples: Earlier we talked about the local Department of Motor Vehicles office. They are easy to pick on because everyone has a horror story. In fairness, however, a great number of dedicated employees work at motor vehicles offices throughout the United States. As the late statistician and international quality guru W. Edwards Deming preached, 98 percent of problems in the workplace, be they customer service or other, are caused not by poor employees but rather by systems and procedures that are flawed. In other words, management is at fault, in Deming's view, and most employees are trying very hard to do a great job in spite of these flawed systems. The problem is, though, that the customer doesn't care whose fault it is. If they receive (or perceive) bad service, they will go somewhere else if they have a choice.

Anyway, back to the DMV. When you visit your local office to renew your driver's license or register your car, what are your expectations for service? Mine are a long wait in line and the strong probability of having to come back a second time with more documentation. In short, my expectations are fairly low. (I actually saw a crude handwritten sign taped to the wall in a local DMV office that said, "We are currently understaffed, and apologize for the length of the lines." "A" for effort on the part of some motivated employee (remember what Deming said), but what kind of perception does that sign create? The good news in this situation is that it doesn't take much to exceed my expectations. Even after standing in line for 45 minutes, if I receive courteous, helpful, and efficient service, I will no doubt leave with a more or less positive perception.

Think of some other service situations in which an expectation was created and the actual experience came up short, causing a disappointment gap. Situations such as:

★ You go see a play at your local community theatre, one that all your friends have been raving about so you are psyched. That evening, try as you may, you don't particularly enjoy the play. It's not that the play was a bad one (it received rave reviews), it's just that your perception of it was not good. Are you a bit disappointed? Yes. Are you more disappointed than if you had walked in off the street at the last minute with no expectations as to the quality of the production? Probably so, because the disappointment gap (between expectation and reality) is greater.

★ A department store has been advertising a sale (when aren't they!) with a deep discount on an item you really want. Your expectations are high. You go to the store and they are either sold out or are out of the model you want, your size, etc.

Your disappointment is immediate. Now, the disappointment gap will be narrowed a bit if the store offers you the sale price when the item comes in, as they often do. Still, you are disappointed because your expectation level has been elevated through advertising, and you feel that you have wasted a trip.

★ A parts supplier that your company has been dealing with for years, and which enjoys an excellent reputation, delivers a crucial shipment two days late causing you to miss a production deadline and delay a shipment to an important customer.

Map the Gap

Think of both a personal and a business example for each CARE Factor where you had a high expectation set, only to find that the actual customer experience fell short, resulting in a disappointment gap.

Competition
Advertising
Reputation
Experience

Service Is Defined by Customers

Exactly what do customers want in the way of service? It's important for you as service providers to fully understand how customers define quality customer care, because it is against these criteria that perceptions are formed and judgments made. A considerable amount of research has been done on the subject. A survey of several thousand customers conducted by the Marketing Science Institute in Massachusetts and reported in the book *Delivering Quality Service* revealed the following five dimensions to quality customer care:

---

1. Reliability
2. Responsiveness
3. Assurance
4. Empathy
5. Tangibles

---

1. **Reliability**—Stop and think for a minute of the businesses you frequent on a regular basis, whether it be for preparing your tax returns, getting your automobile serviced, sending an important document by overnight carrier, or entertaining an important client at a business lunch. What factor, more than any other, makes you loyal to that business? Chances are it's reliability. If your product or service is not reliable in the eyes of the customer, you may as well put out the for sale sign. In the words of former football star and sportscaster Don Meredith on *Monday Night Football*, "Turn out the lights, the party's over."

Reliability, meaning you are consistent and you follow through, is the ticket of admission to today's competitive arena. Being reliable alone won't get you more customers, but without it you will lose customers faster than you can count. Reliability can also be defined in terms of the "grandmother rule":

★ Do what you say you are going to do.
★ Do it when you say you are going to.
★ Do it right the first time.

Most of us were raised with those kinds of values. That's why we call it the "grandmother rule." Customers expect, in fact demand, the same, and will absolutely walk if they even perceive your organization is not reliable. Put another way, can your customers trust you?

A good example of this is repair service for office equipment. Most retail businesses and professional and government offices depend heavily on quick-copy and fax machines to produce and send the reams of paper that, in spite of technology, is still the commodity that fuels every transaction. Who has not endured the frustration of hurrying to the copy machine only to find a crude, handwritten note, "OUT OF ORDER," taped on the top?

Your first question? "Has anyone reported it?" With today's flatter organizations, you may not even get an answer to that question. If you are lucky enough to have an office manager, chances are a trouble call was made, but who knows when a repairman will arrive.

Reliability in this case means getting a repair technician on site quickly, or at least within the time frame established in the maintenance contract.

What happens when you buy a piece of furniture for your home and need to have it delivered? Most stores give you a day and a window of time (usually four hours) during which the furniture will be delivered. It's bad enough that you have to sit in your house waiting for four hours (exceptional customer service delivery would narrow that window considerably). But if you have to wait beyond your assigned delivery time frame, you are not real happy with the reliability factor! Next time, you may just take your business elsewhere.

2. **Responsiveness**—Let's assume your business has passed the reliability test—your product and service is consistent, and you follow through on your promises. The next test of your ability to survive in the long term is responsiveness to the needs and wants of your customers. As a service provider, responsiveness means being absolutely tuned into the needs of your customers and then taking action to meet and even exceed those needs. I recently went into my bank over the noon hour to conduct several transactions that couldn't be performed at an ATM. One customer was being served, and I was the only person in line when I arrived. Five tellers were on duty, while I waited five minutes to be summoned to the one teller who was accepting customers (the others were counting their money or talking among themselves). I pointed this out to my teller, who replied in a frustrated tone, "I know . . . it's ridiculous!"

By the way, those customer needs and wants have become a lot more demanding through the years. Dr. John Pickering, of the Commonwealth Center for High Performance Organizations at the University of Virginia, describes the evolution of customer wants in terms of three attributes:

Quality—I want a good product or service.
Price—I want the product or service cheap.
Speed—I want the product or service fast.

If we look back over the history of the last century, according to Pickering, we find that around 1900 a "pick one" mentality existed in this country. Business at that time could distinguish itself and find a customer base by providing only one of the above three attributes. Henry Ford initially was satisfied with just cheap. The main goal was to ensure that every family in America could afford an automobile and that the company made a profit. He was not interested in good to the same extent. Cars in those early days were not terribly reliable, and there was little if any choice of models. "You can have any color, as long as it's black." Neither was speed a major focus of Henry Ford. Production lines proceeded at a slow pace. You got a car when one became available.

By the early 1970s, advancing technology and customer attitudes allowed a shift from a "pick one" to a "pick two" mentality. We could get our product or service good and fast at the expense of cheap, or good and cheap at the expense of fast, or fast and cheap at the expense of good. It was very difficult as a customer to get all three. And, with little international competition, "pick two" was good enough for most U.S. businesses to flourish.

By the mid to late 1970s, with the onslaught of worldwide competition, "pick two" no longer was good enough. Business models and processes being developed in Western Europe and the Far East were based on "pick three"—good, fast, and cheap. In industry after industry, the United States continued to fall behind. In some markets, such as consumer electronics, we all but disappeared. In others, such as photocopiers and automobiles, we made a recovery but learned some hard lessons. As we enter the twenty-first century, "pick three" is a necessary ingredient to business survival. In our world of direct customer care, "pick three plus" should be our standard! The plus in this equation is value. Customers in today's marketplace want to pay a fair and reasonable price but are often willing to shell out a little more for value—which can be defined as exceptional customer care.

3. **Assurance**—Just as customers are looking for the best value for their money, they also want to feel they are valued by service providers. They want to feel they are important and are not simply a

number or statistic. Personalized service is another way of putting it. Here are a few examples:

★ When you call Great American Business Products in Houston, Texas, and are put on hold, you are told to ask the customer care representative for a free gift because of the inconvenience.

★ A furniture store in the Southeast rolls out a red carpet from their delivery truck into your living room as soon as they arrive at your house.

★ The veterinarian who calls your house the evening after she's treated your pet, just to make sure Angus is doing OK; or the orthodontist who calls a couple days after he has put new braces on your son, just to check that they aren't too tight and causing discomfort.

Mini-Exercise

Think of the last time you felt truly valued as a customer. Jot down the experience in the space below.

_____

_____

_____

How can you make your next customer feel truly valued?

_____

_____

_____

---

4. **Empathy**—Of all the ingredients to exceptional customer care, empathy is perhaps the most important yet the most lacking tool in the arsenal of service associates. Not only do customers want to feel important, they want to feel that somebody sincerely cares about them and their concerns. They want to know that you are on their side, that you under-

stand their point of view. One reason empathy is in such short supply is simply that it is not a skill that can be laid down in a policy or training manual or easily taught as part of customer care orientation. It is one thing to teach associates to answer a phone within three rings or say "please" and "thank you." Empathy is something that must be deeper. It must come from inside people. Do you really care about your customers? Is it in your heart to provide exceptional service? Do you actually want to treat customers in a caring way? Associates who can honestly answer yes to these questions are truly committed to service and not merely following policies.

THE COLD SHOULDER

A woman was mugged on her way to work, and her pocketbook was stolen. This particular woman was very conscientious, and so upon arriving at work one of her first calls was to a credit card company. One of the things in her stolen pocketbook was the invoice and payment check. Her voice still shaking, she explained the predicament to the customer service associate who answered the phone. The customer asked if she could have a few more days to make payment without a late charge. The response of the associate went something like, "Uh huh, uh huh, uh huh, so you say you can pay next Friday." No reference to the mugging or empathy for the ordeal this customer had just been through. Just give us our money!

Contrast that situation with a customer care associate working at a call center of another large credit card company who received a very unusual request. One afternoon an elderly cardholder called. It seems that her husband suffered from Alzheimer's disease and had walked out of their home and wandered off. She had no idea where he had gone but knew that he had a credit card in his wallet, which he often used. Could the company possibly help trace his whereabouts? It would have been easy for the associate to say, "Ma'am, we can't help, but I recommend you call the police." That wouldn't have been an inappropriate response. This particular associate, however, felt empathy for this couple and was motivated to do more. She logged on to the company's online transaction tracking system and, sure enough, the gentleman had just made a credit card purchase at a mall about two miles away. Within minutes the elderly gentleman had been retrieved, thanks to the help of a caring call center associate. That's empathy! It is being literally in partnership with the customer. It is not making the customer feel like they are the enemy.

5. **Tangibles**—This fifth dimension is really about the basics, the tangibles. Does your product or service meet my basic requirements? If I'm in a hotel room, is it clean, and can I sleep without being disturbed by noise next door? Does the product I just bought work as advertised? I recently purchased a new lawn mower, the fancy kind that is self-propelled, from a leading retail chain. After the second usage it stopped working completely; it wouldn't start. I loaded it into the back of my car and returned it to the store, grumbling all the way about the incompetence of the manufacturer. When I arrived, I was greeted by a very pleasant and competent sales associate who immediately figured out the problem. He personally unloaded the mower from my trunk, fixed the machine (a belt had jumped the track), explained what had happened and how I could fix it easily if it happened again, reloaded the box in my trunk, and apologized profusely for the inconvenience. Not only was this associate competent, he took ownership of my problem and didn't pass me around. Customers want that. If they are calling, they want to deal with one person. It's called the one voice concept. Ritz-Carlton Hotels has a firm policy that any associate hearing of a customer complaint owns that complaint until it is fixed. Fixing it may involve getting help from other departments, but the responsibility for follow-through and responding to the customer remains with the associate who first learned of the complaint. Unfortunately, we don't see a lot of competency today, so that quality enables us to stand out in a customer's mind.

Think about reliability, responsiveness, assurance, empathy, and tangibles. Together, they shape the first and lasting impression of customers about your organization.

Mini-Exercise

1. Which one of the customer care dimensions listed above do you feel you organization is really good at?

    _____

    _____

    _____

2. Which one is most in need of improvement in your organization, division, or team?

    _____

    _____

    _____

3. If your customers were sitting across the table from you, what would they say you needed to do to make them feel that your organization or team is:

    Reliable _____

    _____

    Responsive _____

    _____

    One that makes them feel valued _____

    _____

    Empathetic _____

    _____

    Competent _____

    _____

    _____

Another Cup of Coffee

As we said earlier in this chapter, Tom Peters first coined the term "coffee stain management" to describe things about an organization that may contribute to negative perceptions in the minds of customers. What are your organization's (or department's) coffee stains? At a local college, where enrollment was declining, a group of faculty and staff members brainstormed a list of coffee stains that were causing prospective students to go elsewhere. Things like:

★ Only one telephone line to the admissions office, resulting in endless busy signals when attempting to get registration information.
★ Financial aid procedures that were cumbersome and definitely not user friendly.
★ Poor traffic flow and signage on the campus (it was easy to get lost).

Once identified, coffee stains can usually be dry-cleaned out. Assemble a team of associates within your organization and brainstorm a list of coffee stains that you feel may be causing negative perceptions by customers. Again, be honest and open.

Exercise

COFFEE STAIN MANAGEMENT

Using a team of associates, identify as many things as possible that may be contributing to a negative perception by customers toward your organization. They may be things such as long lines, faded signs, broken promises, poor telephone techniques, lack of cleanliness, etc. For each coffee stain, list one action you will take to eliminate it.

COFFEE STAIN	ONE ACTION TO FIX
1.	
2.	
3.	
4.	
5.	
6.	
7.	
8.	
9.	
10.	

It's a Wrap

Did you catch all of the following points?

Moments of truth
- ★ It's all about first impressions—positive and negative
- ★ Perception is reality
- ★ Look out for coffee stains

Customer expectations
- ★ Formed based on the C.A.R.E. factors
- ★ Disappointment gap = expectation *minus* reality

What customers *want*
- ★ Reliability—remember the "grandmother rule"
- ★ Responsiveness—tune in to your customers' needs
- ★ To feel valued—not just a number
- ★ Empathy—an inside job
- ★ Competency—attending to the basics

CHAPTER SEVEN

Service with Heart:
The Personal Touch

We begin this chapter with a television commercial. Many of you will remember it, though it never won any
advertising awards. It was a commercial for a major U.S. airline. As the ad unfolds, the sales manager of a firm has marshaled his sales
force for an emergency meeting. It seems the company had just lost a
major client to the competition due to real or perceived (remember perceptions?) lack of personalized customer service. The sales manager is
heard saying, "We've been dealing with our customers by letter, phone,
fax, and electronic mail, and we've lost track of who they really are." The
final scene shows the manager handing out airline tickets to the sales force
to go pay personal calls on their customers, and then flying out himself to

BULLSEYE

try and regain the major customer his company has just lost. While the purpose of the commercial was to promote air travel, the underlying message was much more powerful. In today's fast-paced, technology-driven world, we are losing the personal touch. How many times when making a call, particularly if the news is negative, have we actually hoped that we would be connected with a person's voice mail instead of the real person? It sometimes seems easier to leave that type of message in an anonymous manner, allowing no opportunity for immediate feedback.

We will talk a lot more about the use of voice mail in Chapter 11 on Technology. For now, let's get down to some really basic customer skills—communication. When you think about it, exceptional customer care really means exceptional communication skills—effective listening and clearly articulating your message. Two skills, both different, but both absolutely critical to the communication process.

Let's start with listening because it is through effective listening that you can earn the respect of your customers as well as show that you truly understand and care about what they have to say. Think back over your life and try to identify five people you've known who really listen well. I bet you have a hard time coming up with three. Listening, as opposed to simply hearing, is difficult to do and requires our full attention and concentration. The sad fact of life is that too many of us spend a lot more time talking than listening. There are "interrupters" who cut others off in mid-sentence. There are "motormouths" who don't let others even get started. Then there are the people who look like they are listening but in fact are just waiting for the first chance to express their own views. Other people appear to be listening while they're really just thinking about something else altogether.

As customer care professionals, the need for effective listening is even more important than in many other lines of work. It is very difficult to provide assistance to customers until you have figured out exactly what they need or want. Take a minute and do this exercise. On the worksheet on the next page, make a list of some of the types of actions or decisions you must make in your job that require you to listen carefully and obtain accurate information from a customer. We have provided as an example a customer care associate working in a cellular telephone company call center. The purpose of this exercise is to give you an insight into how much your job really depends on listening and obtaining information from your customers.

XYZ CELLULAR TELEPHONE COMPANY
Customer Care Call Center
Information to Listen For

DECISION/ACTION	INFORMATION NEEDED
Determine who the customer on the telephone is.	Name/cellular phone number Last 4 digits of SSN (or other ID code)
Determine the customer's exact problem.	Is the inquiry related to Billing? Existing service? New service? Equipment problems?
Customer can't operate the telephone.	What brand/model phone? Has customer read the instruction manual? What won't the phone do?
Customer wants more time to pay bill.	Reason payment not made When can payment be expected?
Customer wants a different rate plan.	How many calls/minutes now being used? How much long-distance calling is customer doing?

Your Organization
Information to Listen For

DECISION/ACTION	INFORMATION NEEDED
1.	
2.	
3.	
4.	
5.	

Hopefully, after completing this exercise, you will be convinced of the need for effective listening in your role as a customer care associate. Here are five proven steps that will help you improve.

---

5 Steps to Becoming a Better Listener

★ Be ready to listen
★ Ask the right questions
★ Take notes
★ Show you are listening
★ Restate

Be Ready to Listen

This may seem fairly obvious, but being ready to listen requires total focus on the customer at hand, whether in person or on the phone. You need to block out both internal and external noise before starting. Internal noise is all the self-talk that goes on in your mind. The phone rings and you are right in the middle of a project or busy closing out a transaction with a previous customer. You say to yourself, "I'm not ready for another customer yet," or "I wish this phone would stop ringing," or "Sure is a pretty day outside. I wish I was out there." You need to clear out that internal noise and focus on what the next customer has to say.

Then there is the external noise connected with the environment in which you work. If you're working in a call center, for example, you have the din of other associates around you, the on-hold lights blinking, or some other indication of how many callers are waiting after this one. If you are in a store, at a counter, or other "live" setting, the external noise can be even worse. Customers standing in line, an old friend walking by that you'd really like to have a word with, a coworker coming up to ask you a question, or the telephone ringing while you are trying to serve a customer face to face (we'll talk about that in Chapter 9)—there can be lots of distractions. So clear the internal and external noise and be ready to listen. This may mean having the computer screen cleared of the last transaction and ready in front of you, or clearing your head and focusing on the person in front of you or on the other end of the phone line. The key is to focus.

Ask the Right Questions

Time is valuable, both yours and your customers'. It is important that you do everything possible to ask the right questions and get the information needed quickly and accurately. In general, there are two types of questions—open-ended and closed-ended. Open-ended questions, as the name implies, are phrased in such a way to bring out free-flowing responses revealing wide ranges of information. They encourage the customer to explain, describe, explore, or elaborate. You may want to use open-ended questions early in the discussion or when you are fishing for exactly what the problem is. Some good examples of open-ended questions are:

"How may I help you?"
"Please describe the problem you are having with the . . ."
"Can you explain to me how . . . ?"

Closed-ended questions, on the other hand, should be used to narrow the discussion and bring out specific, detailed information that you need. Think of them much like true-false, multiple-choice, or fill-in-the-blank questions on an exam. The majority of the questions that we ask in normal conversation are of the closed-ended variety. Examples include:

"What is your invoice number?"
"Can you access your voice mail?"
"Did you try installing the upgrade?"
"What time would be convenient for us to come by?" (Wish I heard this question asked more often!)

The above discussion may seem obvious, but sound questioning techniques can save time and increase the quality of the information you are gathering.

Take Notes

In situations where you are dealing with many customers during a short period of time, don't trust your memory—write it down or enter it on a computer screen. Obviously, this is much easier to do if you are on the phone and the customer can't see you writing. Even if you are face to face, take a few notes. It helps you listen better because you are concentrating more. Don't try and transcribe the entire conversation. Listen for key words and phrases and jot them down. Even if you don't need the notes right now, they may come in handy later as you catch up on paperwork.

We also recommend you use some type of standard log, form, or database—don't write notes on yellow stickies and post them all over your desk, computer, and walls. You'll lose them!

If you are dealing with a difficult customer, especially on the telephone, let them know that you are writing down his or her concern. Say something like, "I know this is frustrating, especially after holding this long. I am concerned about the problem, and we're going to look into it for you. I'm writing this down." This practice does two things. It lets the customer know you are really concerned about the problem, and it may keep the irate ones from repeating themselves over and over again.

Show You Are Listening

One of the quickest ways to kill a good conversation is loss of interest or attention by one of the speakers. Have you ever been at a social gathering, in the middle of a wonderful conversation with someone, great eye contact, fully engaged, and suddenly you see the other person's eyes glance over your shoulder to someone else they have just spotted in the room (and want to talk to)? Maybe it happens several more times during the conversation. How do you feel? Deflated? Certainly a little less engaged in the conversation than you were before.

Eye contact is only one method of showing someone you are listening. It's part of what we call "attentive silence." Head nods, posture position, and eye contact are all things you can do with face-to-face customers to show interest and encourage them to give you more information. Since attentive silence techniques are pretty difficult over the telephone, you need to move to what we call "attentive words." Words like "yes, I see," "uh huh," "okay," "I understand." Simply make noise every so often so the customer knows you are still on the line and doesn't have to ask if you are still there. Also, vary your attentive words a little. Don't go, "uh huh . . . uh huh . . . uh huh . . . uh huh." Use attentive words while you are researching information for the customer. Say things like, "that screen is just about to come up," or "I'm still looking for the information." By doing this, you keep the customer from talking and bringing up unrelated issues, which may happen if he or she is uncomfortable with the silence. Be sure to put a little variety into these attentive phrases. We observed one associate in a call center who would repeat over and over, "still checking . . . still checking . . . still checking." You want to sound personal, not programmed.

Restate

In order to be a truly active listener you must be involved in the conversation and make sure you understand, or heard correctly, what the customer was saying. One of the best ways to do this is by restating what you heard the customer tell you. Don't repeat it word for word. That may irritate the person and make them wonder if you were listening in the first place. Just rephrase what you heard them say in your own words.

There is another reason for restating, and it's grounded in human psychology. The average person speaks at a rate of about 250 words per minute, while the average listener can listen at a rate of 450 words per minute or more. This large gap may result in your mind wandering and you missing important information. Ever notice while listening to a speaker that you drift in and out or start daydreaming? Maybe you are thinking of the shopping list or the big weekend you have planned. The reason for this is either that the speaker is boring or that you are hearing at twice the rate that the speaker is talking. Your mind thus has some free time on its hands, and we all know what they say about idle minds! Restating will help you avoid missing information that you may not have heard and allows you and the customer to at least agree on the facts of the situation. For example,

> "Mr. Jones, as I understand it, you are concerned about the length of time it took our repair man to arrive at your house, and would like an adjustment to the bill as compensation."

Notice several things about this restatement. First, the speaker makes no decision or takes no position on the customer's request. That comes later. Second, the speaker restates both the *content* and the *emotion* (upset). It's important to restate both. Listening for emotion, particularly over the telephone, is equally important as getting the facts. We call it "listening around the edges." People sometimes communicate things that don't come out in the spoken word. Things like frustration, anger, excitement, and pleasure come out more in tone of language and body language.

"I Shot the Store Clerk?!"

Words   7%

Tone of Voice   38%

Body Language   55%

As the preceding chart clearly shows, only a very small percentage of communication has to do with the actual spoken words. Many of you are familiar with research done by Albert Mehrabian concerning how we communicate one-on-one with someone (not one on many). Ninety-three percent of any message is communicated through tone of voice and visual elements such as body language and appearance (*how* we say something). Only 7 percent has to do to with *what* you say. Listening around the edges enables you to hear some of the feeling and emotion behind the words your customers are speaking. In the movie *My Cousin Vinny*, there is a key scene where a teenager who had accidentally walked out with a candy bar without paying is suspected of shooting the store clerk. During his interrogation by the small town sheriff, the teen is so incredulous when confronted with the accusation, he blurts out, "I shot the store clerk???!!!" During the trial, when the transcript of the interrogation is read aloud, it is done so in a straight monotone, making it sound like the teen confessed to the shooting rather than expressing shock at having been charged. The same words with a different tone of voice and inflection changes the meaning of the statement dramatically. Remember, if *how* we say something doesn't match *what* we say, people will only focus on the *how* part, and the content of your message will be lost.

Just a few closing thoughts on listening because it is such a critical skill for service providers. There is an old saying that there's a difference between listening and waiting for your turn to talk. Which one is your habit? As we mentioned earlier in the chapter, poor listeners tend to interrupt, talk over, or simply not pay close attention to the customer. This is understandable. If you've worked with customers for a while, you know pretty much what they are going to say—there are definite patterns, be they requests for information, complaints, suggestions, etc. You may be tempted just to listen for the first few words and then start working on a solution or giving a response. Try listening to the entire message. You may gain additional insight on how to sell the customer or how to solve the problem.

The listening tips we have provided will help, but you need to practice. Try doing the exercises at the end of this chapter to further improve your listening skills. Another thing you can do is practice with your coworkers. Several of you get together and think of situations where you need to listen carefully to customers. Then do some role-playing. One of you be the listener, one the customer, and the rest evaluate the practice exercise. Then switch roles and practice again. Practice restating so that it sounds realistic and you are comfortable with the skill. You will be surprised how actually practicing good listening techniques can help when you are on the frontline of service.

The Times Are A'Changin'

Let's look at some other communication skills that really make a difference with customers. The ability to provide service with heart, the personal touch, is an art that we seem to be losing in this country. Many years ago, well before the Internet, voice mail, automated teller machines, large shopping malls, and managed health care, life seemed a lot simpler. We walked or drove to the store, bank, doctor, or wherever, and were greeted by name. Shopping, getting a haircut, or cashing a check was as much a social event as it was a business transaction. People traded stories, talked about the weather, and eventually got around to conducting whatever business they came for. (Some of you reading this are too young to remember those days, you'll have to trust us that it's true or ask your parents). In my neighborhood, only a few blocks from my house, is a corner grocery store called Burbage's. Mr. Burbage has operated his store for over 53 years. In recent years it has become more of a convenience store than anything else, with most customers making quick visits to pick up an item or two they forgot at the grocery store or to visit the fabulous meat department. In years long past, Mr. Burbage recounts, the store was filled with regular patrons doing their weekly grocery shopping and socializing with him and with each other. People would spend an hour or more in the store, and everyone knew each other by their first name. At the checkout line, most people simply put the groceries on their account and received a very simple bill once a month. And if a customer couldn't get to the store, the groceries were delivered.

Today there doesn't seem to be much time for small talk and personal touches. Phrases such as corner store, house call, five-and-dime, and barbershop have been replaced by mega-malls, mega-mergers, home shopping networks, and online banking. As we navigate our businesses through the ocean of changes spurred by technology, massive population growth, environmental and ecological concerns, to name just a few, we need to re-emphasize the personal touch—the one-on-one contact that is the common denominator of all customer service transactions. Following are some communication basics to keep in mind.

Choose Your Words Carefully and Avoid Jargon

Even though words themselves represent only a small percentage of getting a message across, poorly chosen words can kill communication. One of the biggest problems we observe in this regard is the use of jargon—

words and phrases that you and your coworkers understand and use every day that mean absolutely nothing to your customers. Professional people—doctors, attorneys, technical support people, engineers, and accountants—are sometimes notorious for using jargon. Ever hear the phrase, "Can you put it into lay terms?" Guess what, we're the laypeople. If you have to use jargon, make sure you define the word or phrase to your customer so that he or she can explain it to someone else later if need be. Here's a tip to follow, regardless of your profession. When dealing with customers, particularly if explaining a policy or answering a question, pretend that you are talking to yourself. Yes, imagine that you are that customer with little or no knowledge of the topic being discussed. Then talk to that customer as you would like to be spoken to. It's a bit of variation on the Golden Rule.

So avoid jargon and acronyms at all cost. I have great respect for people who can explain highly technical products and services such as computers, consumer electronics, advanced manufacturing systems, medicine, and law in understandable terms. It's part of the personal touch that helps you build a partnership with your customer.

Match the Customer's Speed and Style

This strategy may appear to be unusual. It is extremely useful, however, in gaining rapport and building a connection with the customer. Here's how it works. If you are serving a customer who is speaking rapidly, when it is your turn to talk, adjust your rate of speech to more or less match his. The same applies if the customer is speaking at a moderate or even a slow pace. You probably will find that you are already doing this subconsciously. If a customer is using a very simple vocabulary, modify yours so they will be able to understand your message. If she is talking to you in academic language, you might haul out some fifty-cent words yourself. Obviously, you will never get as slow as certain customers or as fast as others, but simply try and make yourself more like them. Take care not to come across as mimicking them, especially if you are talking with someone with a foreign accent.

You should also match your customer in intensity of concern and emotion. This doesn't mean get angry with them if they are shouting at you. It does mean modulating your voice to reflect your customer's intensity level. For example, responding to a customer who is obviously upset and angry using a soft tone of voice will not be as effective as saying (with an animated expression), "I understand this is a concern. If this had happened to me, I'd be angry also. I'm glad you let us know about this so we can fix it." By matching the customer's speed and style, particularly if they are angry, you can gradually bring them down in intensity by first bringing yours back down. Try it. It works!

Matching the Emotion

If the customer is	You
Natural	Are natural
Angry	Show concern
In a panic	Show a sense of urgency
Friendly	Are cheerful
Overburdened	Show sympathy
Frustrated	Are empathetic

A Picture's Worth a Thousand . . .

Research shows that people understand things more easily when some sort of visual picture is drawn to go along with the words. Help your customers understand in the same manner. If someone is having trouble with the format of a company invoice, for instance, show her one and explain it line by line. If the customer is on the telephone, ask her to please have the invoice in front of her. If you are explaining how to operate a piece of equipment, if appropriate, use a real life example to clarify a point for a customer. Imagine having someone explain over the phone to you how to perform a complex routine on your computer. You could just write the information down then go to your computer and attempt to carry it out. Chances are you'll need to call your friend back for clarification. A better approach is to sit down at your computer and perform the functions as your friend describes the steps. Visual props are a big help in getting your customer to understand the information you are providing.

The Name Is the Game

The dictionary defines the word rapport as "a sympathetic relationship; harmony." I think that is exactly what our customers want, particularly in today's fast-paced world. They want us to establish a personal relationship with them, whether they are a onetime customer or a regular patron. I have frequented the same dry cleaners for several years now. The services offered are pretty standard and the prices are high (that seems to be standard also). They offer drive-through service, which is convenient. What I like about the place, however, is that when I pull up and roll down the window, the attendant always greets me by name. I have no idea how all eight attendants keep track of the thousands of customer names, but I'm impressed. I feel special when I go in there, not just a number in line. I once belonged to a church with over 10,000 members. The pastor greeted everyone by name after Sunday services. That's a real gift!

Customers love hearing their name, and you should use it whenever possible. Stay formal—Mr., Mrs., Ms., Dr.—unless the customer asks you to please call him by his first name. Gateway Computer Company has an interesting twist on names. When you call their toll-free number and are finally connected to a service representative, they say, "Good morning, welcome to Gateway, my name is Julie, what's yours?" You immediately have to make a choice between giving them your first name, last name, both names, or no name. Most customers give their first name, so an informal, personal relationship is established right from the beginning of the transaction. Great idea!

Please, Let's Get Personal

I want to relate an incident that happened recently where personal touch was truly needed but failed miserably. Hurricane Floyd struck the North

Carolina coast in 1999, causing damage and misery along the eastern seaboard. In anticipation of the storm hitting the coast further south, mandatory evacuations were ordered for much of Florida, coastal Georgia, and South Carolina. Over two million people totally clogged the interstate highway system heading north out of the storm's path. What ensued was total gridlock on the highways leading out of some coastal cities. As an example, driving times of 15 to 20 hours for the 200-mile drive from Charleston to upstate South Carolina were not uncommon. In short, it was a nightmare!

Spartanburg, South Carolina, was my destination that day. We had four adults, two dogs, and a cat in one car for 15 hours, mostly stop and go. When I arrived at my destination at 5:30 A.M. the next morning and wearily went into a major motel chain to claim my reserved and guaranteed room, I needed a little personal touch—a little empathy. Instead I was met by a rude front desk clerk who had obviously had a bad night. Before I could even get my name out of my mouth, she began shaking her head, getting ready to say, "We have no rooms." She could not have cared less that I had been driving for 15 hours or that I had a reservation. To her, we refugees were intruders who had ruined her normally quiet graveyard shift. I had to practically beg her to check the computer, which indeed revealed I had a reservation. While I stood at the desk checking in, I heard her tell another customer, "*You people* have been coming in all night, and I don't know what I'm going to do!" She became angry with another patron because he didn't have a pen to sign the credit card receipt. Finally, she told another weary traveler, "You better knock first, because there may already be someone in the room!" Incredible, but true.

Later that day a long line of complaining customers presented themselves to the manager to vent their feelings on the hideous treatment. The point? The reputation of that hotel (and, by perception, the entire chain) was severely damaged by the total lack of a personal touch by one employee. Sure it was a horrible night, with scores of unexpected guests, many without reservations. Does that excuse rude, impersonal behavior? In this case, since the associate was alone, she couldn't get "offstage" to rest, but she certainly could have called the manager, even in the middle of the night, for help.

On a positive note, the motel did something with the feedback. Several weeks later personal letters from the general manager were sent out sincerely apologizing for the "unprofessional and unfriendly" behavior of the employee and requesting the offended patrons not to judge the entire organization by the shortcomings of one.

Whether you manage or work at a hotel, retail store, hospital, computer store, or manufacturing plant, the personal touch *will* make the difference over time in customer retention, and therefore, in the success and profitability of the organization. The key to personalizing your service is, without question, developing powerful communication skills. Listening, speaking, tone of voice, body language, empathy—these are much more than words. To customer Service Stars, they are tools of the trade as important for success as a drawing board to an architect or a scalpel to a surgeon.

≈ 15 minutes

Exercise

EXERCISE: LISTENING TO YOURSELF AT WORK

Instructions: Make as many copies of this form as you need. Over the next several weeks, take time out occasionally after dealing with a customer to fill out this self-evaluation form. The customer interactions may be face to face or over the telephone. Be honest in your self-assessment. Take some time at a team meeting to discuss your evaluations with other team members and solicit their feedback.

On a scale of 1–10, with 10 being the highest, rate yourself on these qualities:

1. Did I project interest and friendliness? 1 2 3 4 5 6 7 8 9 10
2. Did I take the initiative in helping solve the customer's problem? 1 2 3 4 5 6 7 8 9 10
3. Did I use the customer's name at the beginning and end of the exchange? 1 2 3 4 5 6 7 8 9 10
4. Was my overall tone positive, with mostly positive word use? 1 2 3 4 5 6 7 8 9 10
5. How much of my tone was negative? Less than 33% negative word use? 1 2 3 4 5 6 7 8 9 10
6. How was my body language? Did I allow it to give a negative perception to the customer? 1 2 3 4 5 6 7 8 9 10
7. Did I listen a lot and let the customer do most of the talking? 1 2 3 4 5 6 7 8 9 10
8. Did I show empathy for a customer when it was called for? 1 2 3 4 5 6 7 8 9 10
9. Did I avoid using jargon or terms my customer couldn't understand? 1 2 3 4 5 6 7 8 9 10
10. Did I thank the customer for his or her business? 1 2 3 4 5 6 7 8 9 10

It's a Wrap

Did you catch all of the following points?

Listen to the voice of the customer
- ★ Listening *versus* hearing
- ★ Five steps to becoming a better listener
  - Be ready to listen
  - Ask correct questions
  - Take notes
  - Show you're listening
  - Restate what you've heard
- ★ Listen to tone of voice and body language

The communication basics
- ★ Watch your words and avoid jargon
- ★ Match the customer's speed and style
- ★ Match the intensity of concern and emotion
- ★ Visual aids help
- ★ Let's get personal—name-calling is good (the customer's, that is)

★ ★ ★ ★ ★

CHAPTER EIGHT

Telephone Skills: The Circular Call

Telephones—we can't live without them. In today's world it's often hard to live with them. I recently tried to contact the client services department of a large company in New York City. After dialing the number and working my way through the automated attendant menu, I finally reached my third taped message. It went like this:

"Welcome to the client services department. We know your time is valuable. We want to help you as fast as we can. This message will be repeated. If your call is not answered, you will be automatically transferred to voice mail and someone will get back to you within three business hours."

Those are the exact words. I wrote them down. The message is a great one; very responsive and promising not to leave me on hold forever. It

BULLSEYE

even admits that my time is valuable! Here's the problem. The voice mail option never kicks in. I listened repeatedly to the recorded voice tell me that my time was valuable and how they want to help me. Their grade? An A for effort and an F for execution.

In Chapter 6 we talked about first impressions and about "coffee stains" that turn customers off even before they get to know you. The telephone is certainly one of the biggest opportunities that customers have to form perceptions, either positive or negative, about your organization. In many cases the phone is the first contact that customers have with your business. And in the age of automated telephones, it doesn't take much to be a hero—simply have a live voice answer. Customers will be thrilled.

A new call center on the East Coast set one of its primary service tenets in its call centers as answering each call with a live voice after the first ring. Ambitious goal! Although they don't always achieve that goal, particularly during peak call periods, when they do, customers are impressed.

In this chapter we will talk about telephone skills. Most of you reading this book spend a lot of time on the telephone and probably talk with a lot of customers (and potential customers) every day. Each call is an opportunity to do one or more of the following:

* Provide information and assistance to a current customer or client, thus enhancing their loyalty to your organization. If the customer is unhappy, the call may mean the difference between retaining or losing that person.
* Gain a new customer or client for your organization. In many businesses, particularly in service industries, potential customers shop around using the phone book, newspaper ads, or recommendations from friends. These "cold calls" are opportunities to distinguish your business from the competition and perhaps gain a customer for life.
* Sell additional products or services, either improved/enhanced versions (upselling), or related ones (cross-selling). For example, a customer inquiry to a pest control service about a onetime spraying may lead to an annual maintenance contract. An inquiry to a bank about current interest rates could result in a new account or other financial services.

To emphasize the power of the telephone and the importance of good telephone skills, we urge you to maintain a log for a day or two similar to the following one. The log will enable you to keep track of the types of calls you are receiving as well as opportunities to gain new customers or sell additional products or services. You might be surprised at the positive impact you make on the business by utilizing the telephone effectively.

Customer Name:_____ ❏ Internal ❏ External
Contact # _____
Other Contact _____
Notes: _____
_____

Referred to: _____
Follow-up Needed: _____

Customer Name:_____ ❏ Internal ❏ External
Contact # _____
Other Contact _____
Notes: _____
_____

Referred to: _____
Follow-up Needed: _____

Customer Name:_____ ❏ Internal ❏ External
Contact # _____
Other Contact _____
Notes: _____
_____

Referred to: _____
Follow-up Needed: _____

The Circular Call

Think of each telephone call you receive (or make) in terms of four critical stages: greeting, gathering, responding, and renewal. The length of each stage will vary according to the type of call; however, in no case should a step be omitted. Each serves a different purpose and each is important to the success of the call.

The Circular Service Contract

Greeting	Renewal
Gathering	Responding

GREETING

In every telephone call, the greeting sets the stage. Whether you are initiating or receiving the call, there are some basics you should observe:

1. **Remember the 3 Ps.** Be pleasant, professional, and positive. If you do nothing else, follow the 3 Ps. Post this phrase above your phone: "Smile. They can hear it." Think of telemarketing calls you receive at home for a minute. We all get a lot of them these days. Some of you reading this book are making those calls. Each of us has a different tolerance level for telemarketing calls. Some people I know hang up immediately. Others listen to part of the message then quickly end the conversation. Still others hear out the entire message before deciding how interested they are.

2. **Speak clearly.** Enunciate your greeting so the listener can hear what you said. There are few things more annoying than callers running the words in their greeting together so it sounds like mush. One of the reasons this frequently happens is the greeting is too long. We try to squeeze in the time of day (good morning, afternoon, etc.), the name of the business, sometimes a tagline,

("Where service is our middle name"), our name, and a greeting such as "How may I help you?" The resulting greeting may be quite lengthy, and in our haste to get through it we run the words together. This is deadly because it kills the sincerity of the greeting. Review your greeting carefully, eliminate any unnecessary phrases, and then enunciate clearly and with enthusiasm.

3. **Respond to the caller by name.** We talked earlier about people liking the personal touch of hearing their name. If you are initiating the call, you will obviously know the customer's name. If you receive a call, listen carefully for the name and respond at your first opportunity using the last name. Be careful of pronunciation, however. If the name is difficult to pronounce and you are not sure about it, clarify with the customer. They will appreciate your interest in getting their name correct.

Here are some additional tips to follow for the greeting stage of the call:

★ Check your mood, energy, and attitude. Before you pick up the phone, give yourself a quick attitude check and summon your energy. Remember, on the phone a lot of the energy level you may have gets lost in the telephone lines. You have to make an extra effort to convey enthusiasm and vigor.

Notes

Note to managers and team leaders: You may want to consider getting a tape recorder to allow your associates to tape some of their actual customer conversations. Let them listen to the tapes privately as feedback on such things as rushed greeting, lack of energy and enthusiasm, tone of voice, and other important elements of the phone conversation.

★ Assess your caller. What's their mood? Angry? Frustrated? Frantic? Calm? Listen for words, tone, and inflection. Many customers are direct and to the point. They have no particular mood; all they want to do is transact their business with you, get off the phone, and get on with the next task. "What's my balance?" Be sensitive to those types of callers as well.

★ React with sensitivity. Tailor your greeting to the mood of the caller.

★ Empathize with their need to call you. Let's say you work in the claims processing section of an automobile or home insurance company. Not many people will be calling you in a great mood! Most were just in an accident, suffered damage to their home through fire, tornado, hurricane, or other natural disaster, or were just robbed. Do you think a little empathy is needed in those situations?

TRANSFERRING THE CALLER

Part of the greeting stage is a decision on whether it is necessary to transfer the call. You answered it, but you may not be the one who can help the customer. In general, it is best not to transfer callers, especially if they've already told their story to someone else. Customers in today's world don't want to deal with another person. They want just one voice. They want you to take ownership of their problem or request.

Nonetheless, it is necessary from time to time to transfer callers. Here are some do's and don'ts:

Transferring a Caller

1. State what you **can do**, not what you **can't.**
2. Avoid using the word **transfer.**
3. Brief your coworker before passing the call.

---

1. State what you can do for the customer, not what you can't. For example, instead of saying, "I can't help you, but I'll transfer you to Mary, say, "I can help you by letting you talk to Mary. She'll be able to help you with that." Almost the same words but a much more positive message.

2. Avoid using the word transfer. Instead say, "Let me connect you with Mary," or, "Let me put you in touch with John." The difference is subtle, but the word transfer has a finality to it that may give the customer the feeling he or she is about to be dropped into a dark hole. Remember, perception is reality. "Why don't I let you talk with Susan" is more positive and gives the impression, at least, that the person you are transferring them to is right across from you.

3. Brief your coworker before transferring the caller. Summarize the conversation and let the customer know you've done so. Have you ever been transferred one or more times trying to get some information only to have to start over with each succeeding person in explaining the reason for your call? It's frustrating, and it eats up valuable time for you and the customer.

A good transfer would go something like this:

Associate 1: "Mrs. Jones, why don't I let you speak with Mr. Johnson. I'm going to brief him on your question before he picks up so he will be better able to assist you. May I please put you on hold?" (Obviously you can only do this if you know Mr. Johnson is available. Under no circumstances should you ever "dump" a caller into someone else's voice mail during the transfer process. The term "dumping a call" is widely used in the call center industry to describe the practice of relegating callers to telephone cyberspace. Needless to say, "dumping" and exceptional customer care don't exactly go together.)

Associate 2: "Good afternoon, Mrs. Jones, this is Mr. Johnson. Thank you very much for holding. I understand you have a question about our sales returns policy. How may I help you?"

Again, it would be better if associate number one can answer the question, but that's not always possible. Should you have to transfer a caller, at all costs avoid doing it more than once. If you cannot help the customer after two tries, take his or her number and call back with an answer. You should also review your policies and procedures to determine why it took so much effort to answer the question. It would also be wise to make a written note of such difficult to answer questions and utilize the feedback later to determine if a trend exists. For example, if corporate headquarters made a minor revision to the format of the invoices it was sending out and forgot to inform associates in the field, you may receive inquiries from customers about the changes. If you are keeping track of these questions, you and your fellow associates should quickly discover the trend and request clarification from the home office.

GATHERING

Once you have properly greeted the customer and set a positive tone for the phone call, it's time to get to work answering the question or solving the problem. Before you can do either, you must gather as much information as possible from the customer. Refer back to the last chapter on listening skills, because that's what you are doing in this stage of the call. Here's a review of the basics:

- ⋆ Be ready to listen
- ⋆ Be ready to take notes
- ⋆ Show you are listening through attentive silence and attentive words
- ⋆ Ask questions
- ⋆ Restate what the caller said in your own words

RESPONDING

After listening carefully to the customer's question, problem, or angry statement and understanding what issue needs to be addressed, it is time for you to respond. In general, you have two options for this stage of the call:

1. **Answer the customer's question or solve the problem immediately.** This is the best option. Time and experience with your organization, ongoing training in products and services, and clearly articulated and publicized policies and procedures are all factors that will increase the percentage of calls you will be able to resolve immediately by yourself. We all know the sense of

frustration and helplessness we feel when new in a job and every telephone inquiry is an adventure. We know enough to be dangerous in those first few months, and it seems that every call ends up being transferred. Telephone call centers realize this and most don't put new associates on live calls for some period after they start. At National Car Rental's reservation centers, for example, new associates work in an area known as "the bridge," where the ratio of associates to supervisors is four to one. Live customer calls are fielded by these new associates; however, help is just seconds away.

2. **Place the customer on hold and seek a quick answer from a team leader, or someone in the know.** Like it or not, you won't be able to answer every customer question based solely on your knowledge, experience, or the notes in front of you. Remember that someone around you does have the answer. To get answers for your callers, you must first buy some time by placing them on hold. Before requesting assistance, be sure the information the customers need isn't right in front of you. In most cases today, you will have a number of automated databases available at your fingertips. Use them! If you can't find the information, ask a coworker or team leader.

WILL YOU HOLD, PLEASE?

Here are a few tips for placing a caller on hold.

- **Ask for permission.** "Will you please hold?" Or even better, if you have been talking with the customer for awhile, "Mr. Brown, would you mind holding for a moment while I get an answer to your question?"
- **Wait for the response.** Don't push that hold button until the customer says yes to your request. There is another reason for this besides common courtesy. The customer may not have time to wait and would rather you research the problem and call them back. At least give the customer the option.

- **Watch the clock.** Don't ever leave someone on hold for more than 45 seconds. If you don't have an answer in that period of time, come back on the line and provide an update. If customers have something to listen to like soft music (no promotional ads, please) and get an update regularly, they will stay on hold a little more patiently.
- **"Thank you for holding."** Say this each time you come back on the line. Don't say, "I'm sorry you had to hold." In the first place, you're not really sorry, and secondly, if they are unhappy with holding, you give them an opening to vent their feelings. "You should be sorry! Every time I call this sorry company, I get put on hold!!!!" Don't let the customer even go there.

RENEWAL

The final stage of the telephone call is one that very few businesses train their associates to take full advantage of. That's a shame, because it is as important as the greeting, perhaps even more important. Just as the greeting sets the tone and provides a first impression for the caller, the renewal presents an opportunity to create a lasting impression that may mean the difference in retaining the customer. Think of the renewal phase as your opportunity to invite the customer back. Here are some tips on closing out a telephone call.

- ⋆ **Be personal, not programmed.** How many times have you been talking on the telephone with a company representative and the call ends with something like, "Thank you for calling XYZ Company, haveaniceday" (pronounced as one word). Click. What lasting impression does that leave with you? You can almost picture someone sitting at a desk somewhere with a telephone headset on and dozens of hold button lights blinking in front of him.
- ⋆ **Stay away from standard closures.** At least stay away from closures that sound standard. Most telephone call centers, for example, develop scripts for their associates to follow, particularly

in the opening and closing phases of the call. While these standard opening and closing phrases ensure consistency in the message from one associate to the next, they can sound deadly dull to the customer. Service Stars find a way to inject a bit of their own personality into the script, even if just in tone of voice or inflection. I have been on the phone with call center associates who, once they found out where I lived, made some reference to having visited my city or having relatives here, or simply saying, "I would love to visit your city sometime. I've heard it's a great place." Whether you have any intention of ever visiting isn't important. The important thing is to make a personal connection with the customer.

✴ **Ask if anything else is needed.** Always end calls by asking customers if there is anything else you can help them with. This serves two purposes. First and foremost, it lets the customer know you are interested, not in a huge hurry to get off the line (even if you are), and want to help as much as possible. Secondly, it may lead to more business for your company. When you call an 800 number to reserve a room at a major hotel chain, how do call center associates almost always end the call? "May I help you with any other reservations today?" or, "Do you need a rental car for your visit?" Obviously, they are not saying those things just to help you out. They want your business!

✴ **Repeat your name.** One of the last things the customer should hear is your first name repeated over for them. "Again, my name is Kim, and if there is anything else I can help you with, please call again." Chances are, if they ever call back, they won't remember your name and will be dealing with another associate. That's not the point. Remember, you are trying to connect with the customer, inject your personality into the call, and establish a positive perception in the customer's mind about doing business with your firm.

And finally, the most important stage in the renewal process:

✴ **Thank them for their business, and thank them personally.** "We're so pleased you chose us for your Internet service." "I see that you have been a customer for three years and know that you have plenty of choices. Thank you for continuing to do business with us." These and other similar closings serve to renew the important relationships with your customers each and every time they call.

A Few Closing Thoughts

Many of you spend a large portion of every workday on the telephone with customers. Most of your phone calls are routine. Some callers are very friendly and interesting; a few are angry, upset, even rude. Regardless of the type of call or caller, remember that for many customers the telephone is the way they form their first impression of the organization you work for and represent.

Telephone skills often become so second nature to us that we forget to pause, sit down, and reflect honestly on how we come across over the phone lines. We urge you to take the few tips we have provided in this chapter to heart. Post them over your phone and think about them from time to time. They will help you be a true professional on the phone.

EXERCISE: EVALUATING YOUR TELEPHONE TECHNIQUE

Exercise

Instructions: Give this form to a coworker or team leader and ask them to fill it out while monitoring your telephone technique. After the call is complete, ask them to review the evaluation form with you.

Assoc. Name: _____ Date: _____ Evaluator: _____

CIRCULAR CALL	E	A	MS	NI	U	NOTES
A. Greeting						
Proper Greeting						
Professional						
Positive						
Empathetic						
B. Gathering						
Readiness						
Listening Skill						
Key Fact Find						
C. Review/Respond						
Restate Need						
Offer Assistance						
D. Renewal						
Resolution						
Step Up						
Thank You						
Proper Close						
E. Total Score						

E = Exceptional A = Above Average MS = Meets Standard NI = Needs Improvement U = Unacceptable

Call Acuity:	Easy	1	2	3	4	5	6	Difficult
Customer Began:	Positive	1	2	3	4	5	6	Negative
Customer Ended:	Positive	1	2	3	4	5	6	Negative
Closure in One Call:	Yes	No						

It's a Wrap

Did you catch all of the following points?

The telephone . . . what an opportunity to

★ Provide information and assistance
★ Gain new customers
★ Up-sell and cross-sell

The Circular Call

Greeting—sets the stage

★ The three Ps: pleasant, professional, positive
★ Speak clearly and be concise
★ Use the customer's name
★ "Attitude check" before picking up the phone
★ Transfer calls with care

Gathering—get to work

★ Listen, listen, listen
★ Information is gold
★ Take good notes

Responding—you have options

★ Answer the question/solve the problem immediately
★ Place customer on hold and find the answer
★ "Will you hold, please" tips

Renewal—create a lasting impression

★ Be personal
★ Avoid standard closures
★ "How else may I help you?"
★ Thank customers for their business

Customer Right-eousness: Dealing with the Challenging Ones

How many times have you heard the phrase "the customer is always right"? Whoever said that never had to deal with customers! Many times the customer is not right (or at least not correct). Chances are they were unaware of or misunderstood a policy, didn't realize that half of the shift called in sick or that the computer system was down, or overlooked any number of operational problems that haunt businesses every day. Perhaps a more accurate statement might be, "the customer is always the customer." You see, the customer always *thinks* he or she is right, and that is all that matters in the customer service business. If we want to keep customers coming back, we must treat that perception as reality.

The fact of the matter is that most customers are great. They are friendly, understanding, and tolerant. They are also knowledgeable, demanding, conscious of the value of their time, and hold high expectations for quality of product and service. You as service providers should never take these customers for granted. They are the ones who make your jobs rich, rewarding, and, hopefully, profitable. On the other hand, if you didn't have some tough, challenging customers to deal with, wouldn't life be a little bit boring? OK, maybe that's a stretch. Like it or not, however, you need to be prepared for the inevitable. Even when customers are wrong, you must respect their perception and treat them with respect.

Before we give you some tips on dealing with your challenging customers, you need to know why customers get angry in the first place. To do this, it's probably helpful to turn the tables and put yourself in the place of the customer. You are, after all, a customer too! What makes you angry or upset? Chances are the same things that press your hot button have the same effect on your customers. By focusing a bit on these issues you can reduce the stress and headaches that come with unhappy customers. Let's look at a few reasons customers become upset with a business (and usually take it out on the frontline service associate!).

Why Customers Get Upset

★ Expectations not met

★ Someone was rude

★ Someone was indifferent

★ No one listened

---

1. **Customer did not get what was expected.** Put another way, you did not get what was promised to you. I recently contracted to have my two-story frame house spray washed to get rid of dirt and mildew. The house washer, a pleasant, professional young man with a good reputation, arrived early one morning and began the three-hour job. He informed me prior to starting that I might want to put towels around the windows and doors so that the pressurized water wouldn't get into the house. No problem; I followed

him around the inside of the house with towels as he washed out-side and no water got in. About 24 hours after the house was cleaned (it was spotless!), I noticed that most of our plants and shrubs were dying. When I called the company, the gentleman informed me that due to low water pressure in my housing area, he had doubled the bleach solution to compensate and make sure that the upper part of the house was cleaned. I had the cleanest house on the block, but the landscaping looked like a nuclear winter had set in. I certainly didn't get what I expected.

Same song, second verse. Have you ever pulled into a motel after a long day's drive and gone inside to register (armed with your confirmation number) only to discover that the motel is not holding a reservation for you and that all of the rooms are booked? Fortunately, this doesn't happen often, but when it does, and your expectation is not met, anger and frustration are the order of the day.

I recently experienced the opposite situation at a Hampton Inn in Savannah, Georgia. Upon checking in, the desk receptionist politely informed me that the motel did have my reservation and a room ready. It seems, however, that three busloads of high-school students on a senior trip were about to descend on the hotel. The receptionist offered me a complimentary room at a comparable motel several blocks away. That's an expectation met and exceeded! Had the offer not been made (and readily accepted!), I would have been calling the front desk at two in the morning angrily asserting my rights as a customer.

Thousands of examples could be given of expectations not met. Who hasn't been in the drive-through lane of a fast food restaurant, ordered and received food, driven home, opened the bag, and discovered either wrong or missing items? Your anger and frustration over not getting what you expected are immediate. Or which one of us has not pulled a freshly cleaned and pressed shirt out of the plastic bag only to have a button crumble in our hand!

The solution? Raise the quality of your product or service or, in some cases, make sure the customer is clear in advance on what to expect. Think back to my house washing experience. I could have covered my plants with plastic had I known they were in imminent danger of extinction! As for the Hampton Inn manager, he not only made clear to me what to expect (noisy teenagers), but took it one step further by offering an attractive alternative as a way of avoiding an unhappy customer.

2. **Someone was rude.** Nothing can make a customer angry more quickly than rudeness. Many times the customer is perceiving, not receiving, rude treatment. Doesn't matter! Again, perception is reality in the customer service business. A newspaper I write for had an account for years with a photo shop next door. We bought a lot of film and had a lot of pictures developed there. One day, as I dropped off some negatives, the owner told (not asked) me to have our business manager come down and see him about a delinquent invoice. When she arrived in the store a few minutes later, he blurted out (in earshot of numerous customers), "Ah, *Business Journal* bookkeeper accountant lady, come into my office to discuss your account." Was she embarrassed? Was he rude? Did we cancel our account? Did the owner care? The answers are yes, yes, yes, and NO!

Ever been to the refund and exchange desk of a department store on the day after Christmas? It sometimes seems that all rules of civility are suspended for customers and sales associates alike on that day. Or even worse, the customer service desk of an airline just following cancellation of the last flight to Anywhere, USA. With frustration at a fever pitch, and tempers as short as summer in Alaska, the mere statement, "I'm sorry, we've had to cancel the flight because the engine fell off," might be perceived as rude behavior by some.

The solution? Read on. We'll give you some practical advice later in this chapter on how to deal with challenging customers without resorting to rude behavior.

3. **Someone was indifferent.** Have you ever asked a question of a service provider and been greeted with a response such as, "I don't know, I just work here," or "That's our policy." Words,

actions, and attitude of frontline service people frequently communicate a "can't do, can't help you" message to customers.

The solution? Make sure your associates feel like a part of the team and give them the authority and support to make a difference with customers. At Ritz-Carlton, well known for outstanding customer service, every employee at every new hotel hears personally from CEO Horst Schulze about the mission, vision, and values of the hotel, as well as his high service expectations. What's more, Ritz employees, from manager to bellhop, are empowered to make things right for customers, even if it means spending some money to do it. It's a powerful message. And it works!

4. **No one listened.** This is perhaps the most troubling reason of all why customers get upset. By not listening we have wasted an opportunity to satisfy a customer. We have also lost some valuable feedback to improve our products or services. The following letter was actually written by a friend to the corporate headquarters of a home video company. While you can debate the issue of who is right in this situation, the fact is the customer never received a reply to his feedback other than a one-line "Thanks for your letter." That's not listening.

Dear Sir,

It is 9:15 Friday night and I have just gotten home from one of your video stores. Going to this particular location is something that my family and I have done on a regular basis for the last 10 years. When we first started to patronize the store, it was a xxxxxxxxxx Video Store. We chose this store because, unlike the xxxxxxxx Video nearby, this store did not require me to fill out a credit application revealing my personal income for the privilege of renting a videotape. I had, and still have, a difficult time understanding why my personal income is something a clerk needs in order to determine if I am worthy of having ten dollars worth of credit extended to me. Unfortunately, xxxxxxxx purchased the store, but we continued to use it. The reason for this letter is to give you some feedback on how your employees are treating customers.

When I tried to check a movie out tonight, the clerk asked me for my name. After I told her my last name, she asked for my first name. When I told her it was Doug, she asked if it was Louise. To this I responded, "No, that is my wife's name." The clerk then asked me if my name was Mark, to which I answered, "No, that is my son's name." She then informed me that I was not eligible to check out the movie unless she called my wife or son to see if it was all right. It did not matter that I had been checking out videos for 10 years. As you can imagine, I was a bit disappointed in the way I was treated and decided that the time in my life when I had to be given permission for those sorts of things had long passed.

Are your clerks not allowed to practice common sense? I am a 46-year-old, bald-headed, overweight certified public accountant. I have worked in the same job for the last nine years and lived in the same house for 12 years. I hardly have the appearance of someone who would pose a serious threat to one of your videotapes. My income is sufficient to support one son in college and another in private high school. I only tell you that as further indication of my ability to abstain from doing something you might regret if your employee were to rent me a videotape.

Your mission, "To be a global leader in rentable home entertainment by providing outstanding customer service . . ." was hardly furthered by your employees tonight. If you do not believe customer service and common sense are paramount in a service industry like yours, you most assuredly will be in for a long ride. If you are interested in doing something about this all too important shortfall, I will be happy to share with you the name of a person whom, I truly believe, can provide you with valuable insight into how improvements can be made in this area.

Yours truly,

The solution? Listen carefully and with empathy, then do something with the feedback. Refer back to Chapter 7 for some practical tips on listening effectively.

OK, you've done everything possible to be pleasant, to listen, and to meet your customers' expectations, and they are still upset. Now what? Satisfying even the most challenging customers is a critical skill. Most of us are pretty good at dealing with customers when they are rational, reasonable, and logical because we can analyze situations, provide facts, and give information and technical answers pretty well. The problem is that challenging customers don't respond to logic with logic; they respond with emotion. In fact, the more logical we become, the angrier they get. The only solution to this dilemma is to deal with emotions (theirs and yours) first. The brain simply won't process logic until the anger and frustration are put aside. Here is a proven six-step strategy for dealing with challenging customers.

Dealing with Challenging Customers

1. Stay calm yourself.
2. Let the customer vent.
3. Deal with emotion first.
4. Avoid emotional trigger words.
5. Gently confront abusive customers.
6. Delay action or consult a second opinion.

---

1. **Stay calm.** If you can't remain calm in the heat of battle (and often it is very difficult to do), forget the remaining five steps in this strategy. They simply won't work. Here are two techniques for staying calm.

⋆ Remember the acronym STOP.

S—**Signal**. How do you feel when you first start to grow angry? Does your jaw clench or heart pound? Do you feel suddenly warm or experience sweaty palms? These and other feelings are your early warning signs that anger is setting in. Be aware of them.

T—**Take control** by

O—Doing the **Opposite** of your early warning signal. Drink some water, dry your hands, unclench your jaw, or take a deep breath. Deep breathing, for example, keeps your voice opened and relaxed, not rushed and panicky.

P—Finally, **Practice**. Being aware of your early warning signals and how best to deal with them won't guarantee that you stay calm but will sure increase your odds. If you don't know your early warning signals, ask a coworker or family member. They probably do!

★ **Listen to your self-talk.** Remember earlier in the book when we discussed the power of self-talk? When you find yourself dealing with challenging customers, you will really be utilizing those self-talk skills. When confronting an angry or upset customer, it is very likely that you are saying (to yourself) such things as: "Who do they think they are?" "I don't have to stand here and take this," or "I can't believe anyone would keep going on like this." This type of self-talk only serves to make you angry. Try changing that internal voice into phrases such as "This customer must really be having a bad day to be acting like this," or "I hope I don't sound like that when I'm upset." Modifying your self-talk will help you remain calm and logical with even the most difficult customers.

2. **Let the customer vent.** Listen carefully and don't interrupt. Chances are the customer has memorized exactly what he is going to say, so you might as well let him finish. If the customer is in a public place, try to move to a private room and deal with the situation one-on-one. Don't rush this step; you'll know when the venting is finished, usually by an audible outflow of air.

3. **Don't move to logic yet; deal with the customer's emotions first.** Get your customers talking about what's upsetting them. Here are some tips:
   * Show empathy for the situation. "Mr. Jones, I guess I would be upset too if I received a $350 electric bill."
   * Find areas of agreement with your customer. "I know it's frustrating to have to call back for the second time."
   * Restate what you heard them say. "So you're concerned because this is the highest bill you've ever received from us."
   * Thank the customer (yes, thank him) for bringing the situation to your attention.

The goal is to gradually move the customer from an emotional to a logical state of mind.

4. **Avoid emotional trigger words.** All these do are add fuel to the fire and escalate the anger. Have you ever stood in line for an hour or more to renew a driver's license or register your car only to find out that you have to come back with more paperwork? Were you angry when you left? Probably so, but not because you needed more documents but because you were greeted with emotional trigger words such as, "Look lady..." or "It's state policy," Try using calming words and phrases instead.

TRIGGERS	CALMERS
Policy	Here's what we can do
Can't	Can
Sorry	Thank You
No, I don't know	I can find out
But	And
You should have	I understand why you
The only thing we can do	The best option I think

5. **Gently confront abusive customers.** Most of the time we never reach this stage. After trying the previous four steps and the customer is still difficult, gently confront using a calm and helpful tone of voice. Use the customer's name, but gently set limits to the behavior. Here's how it would sound: "Mr. Jones, I really want to help you. As long as you continue to use this language, I am finding it very difficult to help. I can get this taken care of. Will you let me?" In most cases the customer will answer yes, and you can move on to logic. If the customer is still difficult, move on to the next step.

6. **Delay action or consult a second opinion.** If all else fails, call time out. Say something like, "Let me look into this matter and

I'll get back with you in a few minutes." Consult with a team leader or the manager and, if necessary, bring one of them in on the conversation. Some angry customers calm down just because their grievance has been taken to a higher level. Remember, when all is said and done and the situation is resolved, the customer will remember how he was treated longer than the problem itself.

Once you have been successful in calming the customer down, you are ready to move to problem solving. The objective now is to resolve your customer's problem immediately, whether they are on the phone or standing in front of you. Here's a good approach:

★ Put everything else aside and focus all of your experience and your talent on how to fix the problem.

★ If possible, involve the customer in the solution by asking a question such as "What can I do to make this right?" or "How would you like for us to handle this?" You will be surprised at how reasonable the requests will be. In most cases the customer's solution will involve less than you might have offered. And since the customer thought of it, he'll be much happier and more satisfied with the outcome.

★ Offer a solution based on what the customer thinks.

★ Finally, give the customer your personal commitment to his or her satisfaction. Give your name, extension, and days that you work so the customer can contact you with any further questions. This both reassures the customer and gives him a person— you—who knows the history of the situation and with whom they have built some rapport.

On some occasions, no matter how hard you have tried, the situation with a customer has gone haywire and you must deliver bad news. A long-awaited special order item for a Christmas gift has been discontinued by the manufacturer. The shipment of parts to an automobile assembly plant has been delayed because of a truck breakdown.

The telephone installation scheduled for this afternoon will have to be rescheduled because a thunderstorm took down some lines in another area. There are hundreds of reasons! Here are seven suggestions on how to deliver bad news and still keep the customer in your corner.

1. Inform the customer as early in the process as possible. You've heard the phrase, "Bad news is like a dead fish. It only gets worse with time." Most customers are understanding people, *if you keep them informed* in a timely manner.
2. Inform the customer over the phone or in person, not by letter or e-mail. The personal touch is critical at a time like this.
3. Get to the point quickly: "You're not going to like hearing this."
4. Treat the customer fairly. It will be remembered. Spend some time (and even money) fostering goodwill.
5. Apologize sincerely. Thank the customer for their patience and understanding.
6. Ask for another opportunity to serve them in the future.
7. Do not let it affect your interaction with the next customer.

What do you do about customers who are wrong? First of all, of course, you must recognize that customers are never wrong. They may have different expectations or they may have been overpromised and oversold, but they're never wrong. (Don't worry, they'll remind you!) Remember, we began this chapter by saying that customers are not always right or correct. Aren't we contradicting ourselves? Not really! The difference between not right and wrong is in perception. The customer may be absolutely off base in his rationale or assumptions about your product or service. Since he perceives he has been wronged, the burden is on you, the service provider, to make things right if you want to see that customer again. If you don't care, tell him he's wrong and he can take his money elsewhere (but remember how many other people he will tell!).

With that in mind, here are some techniques to use when the customer appears to be wrong.

1. Deal with emotions first. Help the customer vent. This is the time to use calming words rather than trigger phrases discussed earlier.
2. Establish the facts. Use active listening techniques to find out exactly what happened and why the customer is unhappy.
3. Remember that the customer *is always* the customer, even if he or she appears to be wrong.
4. Maintain respect, and by all means, don't try to place blame on the customer.
5. Move to problem solving, and explain your organization's position.
6. Find the best available option. Be flexible and try to arrive at a win-win solution: the organization follows the spirit of its policy, but the customer always gets some concessions.

Throughout this chapter we have talked about dealing with angry or upset customers with a goal of keeping them in our corner (or at least in our store). Once you have lost a customer (or are on the verge), what do you do to recover? Even utilizing all your tools, there are times you simply can't make things right, when your product or service didn't perform as promised and a customer is disappointed. This is where the following recovery skills come in.

Customer Recovery Skills

- ★ Apologize sincerely
- ★ Take responsibility for fixing the problem
- ★ Solve the problem quickly
- ★ Involve the customer
- ★ Do something extra
- ★ Follow up

---

1. **Apologize sincerely.** Customers can tell when you are faking it! All too often the apology comes across as a flat monotone, such as "Sorry about that." This is a time when tone of voice and body

language are all important. Apologize to the customer in the same manner as you would want to receive the apology had you been wronged.

2. **Take responsibility for fixing the problem.** Don't lay blame and don't make excuses, just set about to solve the problem. Many customer-focused organizations have a policy that the associate first hearing of a problem owns it until it is resolved. That may mean getting others involved, doing some research, and then getting back to the customer with an answer.

3. **Solve the problem quickly.** Customers want a resolution to the problem, and they don't want to wait very long for an answer. For example, a customer calls his supplier after having received an invoice with no purchase order number included. A quick response would be, "I'm sorry, let me read that purchase order number to you now," or "I can fax you a corrected invoice or put one in the mail today. Which would you prefer?" Problem solved!

4. **Involve the customer.** Find out what is most useful to them, not what is easiest for you. Notice in the example just given that the supplier involved the customer by asking whether he wanted the new invoice faxed or sent by mail. Involving the customer is easy to do but is a skill often forgotten in service recovery.

5. **Do something extra.** Correcting the problem is not enough. Recognize the "hassle factor" that your customer experienced. A gift certificate, complimentary glass of wine, or deep discount on a price are just a few examples of little extras that don't cost much and make the difference in winning back a lost customer. Here are a few other innovative ideas we have seen for recovering disappointed customers:

   * A dentist's office that gives movie passes to patients who have had to wait an unreasonably long time to be seen;
   * A fast food restaurant that gives a free order of French fries to customers who have been in line a very long time;
   * A department store that takes an additional percentage off the retail price when an item has to be backordered for a customer;

* A copy machine repair company that brings a complimentary case of paper to a business when it has exceeded the estimated repair date and time following a trouble call.

What Can *You* Do?

List below a few extras that you and your organization might offer to disappointed customers to recover their loyalty.

_____

_____

_____

_____

_____

_____

Note to team leaders: What types of extras do you need to make available to your associates so they can recover disappointed customers? What guidelines do you need to give so that associates will know when to use those extras?

6. **Follow up.** Make sure the customer is truly satisfied. Your goal is to get repeat business. Follow-up telephone calls are particularly effective.

Scott Cook, founder of Intuit Corporation, said, "If you can't please your current customers, you don't deserve new ones." Dealing effectively with angry patrons is one of the most important challenges you face in retaining and expanding your customer base. Pay close attention to it!

Exercise

≈ The time needed to complete this exercise is 20 minutes for each section.

EXERCISE: CUSTOMER SERVICE CHALLENGES

A. Working in one or more groups, brainstorm for 20 minutes a list of the worst service experiences that you have encountered as a customer. Summarize your experiences in the box below, then indicate for each situation one of the following reasons people get angry or upset with service.
  * You did not get what you expected
  * Someone was rude
  * Someone was indifferent
  * No one listened

SUMMARY OF SERVICE EXPERIENCE	REASON FOR UNSATISFACTORY SERVICE
1.	
2.	
3.	
4.	
5.	

B. For each situation discussed and summarized in the first part of the exercise, discuss and then list 2 to 3 ways in which the service provider could have better handled the situation or resolved the problem.

Situation (from list in Part A)	How could situation have been better handled?
1.	1.
	2.
	3.
2.	1.
	2.
	3.
3.	1.
	2.
	3.
4.	1.
	2.
	3.
5.	1.
	2.
	3.

Keep these ideas in mind on the frontlines of customer service. Experience is the best teacher!

It's a Wrap

Did you catch all of the following points?

Why customers get upset
- ★ Broken promises and unmet expectations
- ★ Rude behavior
- ★ Indifference: "Sorry, that's our policy."
- ★ No one listened

Dealing with challenging customers
- ★ Stay calm—remember the S.T.O.P. factors
- ★ Let the customer vent
- ★ Deal with the emotion before trying logic
- ★ Gently confront abusive customers
- ★ Get a second opinion
- ★ Move to problem solving

Delivering bad news
- ★ Keep customer informed
- ★ Personal touch
- ★ Get to the point
- ★ Be fair and foster goodwill
- ★ Apologize
- ★ Ask for another chance

Recovering disappointed customers
- ★ Apologize
- ★ Take responsibility
- ★ Solve quickly
- ★ Involve customer
- ★ Do something extra
- ★ Follow up and through

C H A P T E R   T E N

Customer Feedback: Are You Hungry?

et's make this simple. There is only one rule here. *The customer defines your service.* Did you get that? *The customer DEFINES your service!* It sounds simple, logical. Of course you knew that, didn't you? Then why do so many people operate as if *they* define the service? Why do so many service providers fail to ask the simple questions, "How are we doing?" "Are you pleased with our products and/or services?" "What else can we do for you?" "Will you come back to see us again?"

I have talked to countless business owners, executives, and frontline associates who say to me, "We have a good feel for our customers. We just don't get that many calls, letters, or comments. And management sees

every one we do get so that we can keep in touch." Keep in touch! Give me a break. That's like waiting for a plant to die in order to say, "I guess it needed water."

Notes

Note to team members: Getting customer feedback is too often seen as a management responsibility. Isn't it their job to develop customer satisfaction measures? Don't get caught in that trap. You are the eyes and ears to the customer. You see them across the counters, down the aisles, or hear their voices directly on the telephone. You have a great deal of input to offer, so read on and see what you can do. Help turn this type of informal feedback into a more formal system.

Numerous studies over the last several years have reported consistently that only 2 to 5 percent (depending on your industry) of your customers complain voluntarily. Let's be clear on this. This is not 2 to 5 percent of your total customer base. This is 2 to 5 percent of the unhappy customers, the "I had an unsatisfactory (I may not return) experience" customers. So for every letter or phone call you receive from an unhappy customer, picture another 96 walking out without saying a word. That would sure make you take notice.

In today's busy, demand-upon-demand kind of world, you have to beg for feedback. A better way to say this perhaps is that you need to actively solicit your customers' impressions (the good and bad). And you must do it in the most creative, nonintrusive, easy-to-obtain way that you can. And once you have the feedback, you must do something with it. Not next quarter, next year, or next decade, but now.

A good guide to follow is the A, B, C, D method:
A sk for feedback
B elieve what they're telling you
C ommunicate your results
D o something with what you've learned

A = Ask for Feedback

Asking for customer feedback can be done in many ways. It may be formal or informal. It can be in person, by mail, by phone, by e-mail. It can be conversational or statistical. What's important is that you seek it.

A major urban hotel has a program I love. It's called *Elevator Ears*. That pretty much says it. At this hotel, employees are riding up and down the elevators all day long with customers. In fact, they are encouraged to do so. But these employees are trained not to think of the elevator as a way of getting from floor 2 to floor 12. They are trained to think of it as an opportunity to hear from their guests. It's an amazingly simple way to gather information from a somewhat captured audience. And you hear it all: guests who just registered, a couple from the restaurant, a business-woman from the seminar, a golfer, a swimmer, and maybe even a late sleeper. The fact is, these are the people using the hotel services, and they often have comments. Many times these comments are volunteered without asking. Haven't you taken that moment of reflection in an elevator to say, "Boy, am I ready to get to the room. I thought we'd never get checked in." or "I guess that waitress was having a bad day." Or perhaps you've made a comment on the parking garage or the smell of smoke in the hallways.

Employees at this hotel are also trained to initiate a conversation if they do not hear one. Novel idea, isn't it? The employees simply start the conversation with lines like: "How is everyone this morning? I hope you're enjoying your stay at our hotel." And if that doesn't kick it off, the employee may add, "Has anyone tried our restaurant this morning?" or "I see you've been to the health club, how did you find our services there?" Can you just imagine the impression this makes!

To make this even better, as part of the *Elevator Ears* program the hotel has the *Glitch Report*. The *Glitch Report* is a daily reporting of the things heard by the hotel employees. These items are categorized for trending of poor (as well as outstanding) service areas, and discussions are held with the appropriate management and department personnel to work on correcting the service deficiencies. And don't think that this is all the hotel does to gather feedback. They also have:

⋆ a quick survey card in the rooms and at the checkout desk
⋆ a 24-hour hotline for guest service needs
⋆ an in-room TV station with a guest questionnaire
⋆ and as if that weren't enough, a random selection of guests receive follow-up letters thanking them for their stay and requesting their comments.

One of the attributes I like best about the *Elevator Ears* program is that it's not just for hotels. You can take the same principles of employee training for feedback and apply them to hospitals, retail stores, banks, and even doctors' offices. It's a matter of training employees to listen and to report. Can you think of *listening posts* for your business? A *listening post* can be any location where easy dialogue can take place—hallways, waiting rooms, around counters, throughout restaurants, most any public place.

Name three "listening posts" in your organization.

1.
2.
3.

As a team, can you determine a simple but effective way to share comments from your listening post? Suggestion: Give each team member the challenge of recording three observations in a week and then set aside 10 minutes at a team meeting to share the observations. Develop a simple table, and keep a record of the types of comments that you hear. This will help you track any problem areas or items needing attention.

So Who's Asking Whom?

Let's talk a moment about who we survey for service feedback. Who is our customer anyway? Is it:

★ the purchaser of our product or service?
★ family or friends of the purchaser?
★ the end user of our product or service?
★ a former or "lost" customer?
★ our vendors/suppliers?
★ our employees?

A hospital is a good example that illustrates how difficult it can be to define your customer. The most obvious definition in a hospital is the patient. And certainly the patient is an important customer. But did the patient admit himself/herself, or did a doctor direct them to the hospital? Oh, so the doctor is really the important customer. Did the doctor chose the hospital based on services, or was he or she directed by the insurance provider? I see, so now it's the insurance provider. Did the doctor have several choices, and did the physician's staff have influence regarding the hospital they work best with? Did the patient's employer select the health plan, and how did they chose participating hospitals and physicians in their plan? It gets quite complex doesn't it?

One of the more forgotten groups of customers to survey is those customers whom you have lost. By this we mean those customers who once did business with you but are now doing business with the competition. What made them leave? What is the competition doing better? Is there a way to recover their business? By surveying this group of folks you not only learn a great deal about your service *potholes,* but your last message to the former customer was one that you cared! Wouldn't you prefer that this follow-up be the last impression with the customer as opposed to the bitter taste they carry from the poor service that drove them away?

Notes

Note to team leader: An automobile service shop trained its driver for the shuttle bus to solicit questions and debrief customers. "What do you think of our service shop? How friendly were the folks taking your order? Would you recommend us to your friends and neighbors?" Think for a moment. Have you adequately trained everyone who has contact with your customers?

Another effective feedback method involves the use of "lost job" questionnaires. These questionnaires are unique because they are sent to prospective customers. They are especially useful for companies involved with contracting bids and technical proposals. I remember an article in *Inc.* magazine years ago that featured T&K Roofing, a contractor in Iowa who used a very effective lost job survey. You see, many companies believe that they lose bids based solely on price. T&K discovered this not to be true. They found that many of their bids were lost due to other reasons such as follow-through, sales rep inexperience, or lack of knowledge. They gained great insight from their surveys, which helped them to grow despite eight new competitors in their marketplace. Following is the T&K survey questionnaire:

T&K ROOFING COMPANY INC.

At T&K Roofing Company, our number one priority is to provide and deliver goods and services that our clients want and value. By completing this evaluation, you will assist us in assessing why we did not meet your requirements.

Please identify the following items that affected your decision NOT to accept our bid. Please feel free to be completely honest. Your feedback is very important to us, and your responses will remain confidential.

Thank you for your assistance,
Thomas M. Tjelmeland, President

Were any of the following a major factor in your decision NOT to award the contract to T&K?

1.	Price	Yes	No
2.	T&K reputation (integrity)	Yes	No
3.	Service Offerings	Yes	No
4.	Available warranty	Yes	No
5.	T&K location	Yes	No
6.	Project schedule	Yes	No
7.	Roof system requirements	Yes	No
8.	Billing terms	Yes	No
9.	Established relationship with another contractor	Yes	No

10. Please list the main reasons T&K was not selected:

11. (optional) Can you tell us who was awarded the contract?

12. If price was the reason for losing the business, can you tell us by what percentage T&K was higher than the selected contractor?

13. If service offerings and/or capabilities affected the selection, what did T&K not offer that the competition did?

14. If your project is rebid at a later date, would you like us to contact you again? When?

Please rate the effectiveness of the presentation made by our sales representative (1 = lowest rating, 10 = highest rating). This information will be kept confidential from the representative.

15. Receptiveness and understanding of the project requirements and the need of your firm. 1 2 3 4 5 6 7 8 9 10

16. Presentation of T&K Roofing's capabilities, products, service offerings, and recognitions. 1 2 3 4 5 6 7 8 9 10

17. Presentation of Bid Proposal and Project Strategy. 1 2 3 4 5 6 7 8 9 10

18. Willingness and ability to answer all of your questions. 1 2 3 4 5 6 7 8 9 10

19. Professional appearance. 1 2 3 4 5 6 7 8 9 10

20. Demonstrated respect for the competition. 1 2 3 4 5 6 7 8 9 10

21. Timeliness or response time of initial contact until bid presentation. 1 2 3 4 5 6 7 8 9 10

22. How many times after the representative submitted his quote, did he call to see if you had any additional questions? 1 2 3 4 5 6 7 8 9 10

23. Comments/Questions:

We have discussed a number of people you can ask about your service, but now back to you, the employee. Don't you know a great deal about the customer care being provided in your organization? As a frontline associate who works with customers all day long, I bet you have a comment or two. When were you last asked specifically to provide input on service delivery?

The point to focus on here is that every organization has a myriad of customers and people who influence customer choice. A simple annual survey to a primary base of customers and employees is hardly enough, not if you want to truly understand what your customers like and don't like about what you do.

The Best Way to Ask

How best to survey your customers is a question often asked. The answer is somewhat dependent on your company size, the nature of your business, the frequency of your customer interaction, and the depth of information that you are attempting to gather. Customer feedback is usually grouped into one of two categories: quantitative and qualitative.

Quantitative information is that which is of sufficient volume that it has statistical validity. In other words, you can rely on the accuracy of the responses to be a reflection of your total customer base, and you can feel confident in making decisions based on the data provided. As an example, if your quantitative research shows that 89 percent of your customers do not like your automated voice mail system, then you should definitely consider changing it.

Qualitative information is not statistically valid and should be used with caution. It does not project customer trends and behaviors. Some of the best qualitative surveying is what is done face-to-face by simply asking the customers about their experience. Imagine the wealth of feedback if a grocery store manager made a point of asking 10 customers a day about their shopping experience. We're not talking about questions like, "How was your shopping experience with us today?" That's much too vague, open-ended, and it doesn't invite conversation. In fact, it invites a simple "fine" when things weren't fine. Think if the store manager introduced herself and said, "I hope we are stocking everything you wanted. Were we out of any particular items or did you have trouble locating them?" Many questions could be asked, but they should be specific, conversational, and easy to answer.

Another popular qualitative research method is mystery shopping. Mystery shoppers are paid fake customers who are trained to interact with service providers for the purposes of evaluating their performance such as service response time, attitude, and product/service knowledge. They also look at other service attributes such as facility appearance, cleanliness, and signage.

Other qualitative surveying techniques, such as focus groups, are often used to test new ideas, products, or even research questionnaires before they are applied to significant numbers. Your opportunities for qualitative feedback are virtually endless. You should also try customer feedback forums. These are like customer councils. Bring 8 to 12 of your customers together and converse with them about your products and services. Feed or entertain them and most are more than happy to share their thoughts. A simpler idea is to invite customers into one of your company meetings. Ask them to share a little about their businesses and how they perceive your services. Employees love this kind of interaction, and it allows them to put a face and personality with a customer. Customers enjoy the relationship building as well.

Feedback Tools: A Few Examples

Quantitative
★ Telephone surveys
★ Mailed questionnaires
★ Business reply cards (countertop or product insert)
★ Personal interviews
★ Touch-tone phone surveys at call centers
★ Internet questionnaires
Qualitative
★ Focus groups/customer forums
★ Internet chat lines
★ Mystery shoppers and teleshoppers
★ Employee observations

Please recognize that the feedback methods we've discussed range from the very simple to the very sophisticated. Quantitative research is an art and a science, and it is recommended that it be outsourced to professionals for a variety of reasons. First, outside researchers can provide an anonymous and independent voice to your customer. This often helps the customers feel more at ease in being totally candid in their response. Secondly, the research professionals will construct survey tools that do not bias the customer responses with wording that is confusing or leading. Thirdly, the researchers can perform analysis of the data and make recommendations that in-house resources usually aren't equipped to do.

Most importantly, do not overlook the various ways in which research can be conducted. With the Internet explosion, many companies are using Web sites and targeted e-mails to gain customer feedback. Several new Internet service companies have sprung up that solicit online consumer complaints then make that data available to companies and industries. Other companies find that automated phone surveys work for them. Of course, mailed questionnaires, business reply cards, product or bill inserts, and phone surveys are always options.

Many businesses such as hotels, airlines, hospitals, restaurants, and movie theaters have their customers "captured" for a period of time. This can be a great time to access information about the services provided. It's timely and shows that you care. My dry cleaner puts a small slip of paper in with the monthly bill. One month it may be asking questions about the timeliness of service. Another month it may check on any problems with buttons, pressing, etc. Another month will be about the friendliness of personnel. By breaking it down they have a continual message going to the customer that says "we care," and because there are only a few questions, it makes it quick and easy to reply as a customer.

Deliver It

Deliver It is a great campaign that is conducted at Wachovia Bank. I like it because it maximizes employee involvement and interest in customer care. The name, *Deliver It*, does not refer to delivering service as you might expect. It refers to delivering The Promise. The Promise is an oath or cultural code that all employees are expected to know and embrace. It's their way of doing business.

Deliver It is a huge program that requires commitment. It entails training over a three-month period, and it requires active participation by the employees. The program is effective because it:

★ reinforces the bank's Seven Steps to Exceptional Customer Service
★ trains Wachovia employees to be their own mystery shoppers— for the bank's own customer contact personnel, and for other retail operations
★ serves not only as an effective reporting system for service deficiencies, it has a recognition component for outstanding performance as well

Think about it. As a frontline customer care associate, how better to focus on the attributes of exceptional service than to be continually looking for them in the actions of others. And you have to admit, for most of us, there is something fun about mystery shopping. It's like being an undercover detective. And by mystery shopping other retail operations, you get some fresh examples of clueless, complacent (and yes, sometimes exceptional) service to take back and share with your associates.

The survey tools used in the *Deliver It* program are excellent. They ask very specific questions about the transaction taking place. For example, for a telephone mystery shop, the transaction asks, "If you were placed on hold, did employee ask permission?" and "How long was the hold?" Each answer is given a numerical rating such that total scores can be quantified. This allows rankings to be assigned at the branch bank level and serves as the basis for individual and branch rewards!

Another program similar to *Deliver It* is used by a large parks and recreation commission for their numerous park sites and activities. In their newsletters to park members, they ask for volunteers to serve as mystery shoppers to help evaluate the quality of their services. Additionally, park employees can sign up for the program to mystery shop activities outside their own area. Incentives are offered with free passes to special programs, and the response is wonderful. The volunteers are brought together for initial training and then sent to the field. Some critics may say that these types of in-house programs are not advisable. After all, the mystery shoppers are not trained professionals. We are all consumers, and with proper selection and training, the benefits of employee (and membership) involvement far outweigh the potential concerns.

Exercise

Allow 15 minutes to complete design of Mystery Shop form.
Allow 15 minutes in team meetings for Story Telling.

EXERCISE: I'VE GOT YOUR NUMBER

A. Using the following template, design your own mystery shop form. Make it a simple form that relates to the type of business you do. Substitute any service attributes that are key to the care you provide your customers.

MYSTERY SHOP: I'VE GOT YOUR NUMBER

Shopper Name: _____ Date: _____

Business Name: _____

1. Was I greeted in a warm and welcoming way that made me feel special?   Y / N / NA
2. Did the employee introduce himself/herself?   Y / N / NA
3. After telling the employee my name, did he/she use my name?   Y / N / NA
4. Did the employee listen well to what I needed?   Y / N / NA
5. Was the employee knowledgeable about the products/services?   Y / N / NA
6. Did the employee use good eye contact?   Y / N / NA
7. Was the appearance of the employee professional/appropriate?   Y / N / NA
8. Did his/her body language indicate enthusiasm and interest?   Y / N / NA
9. Was the employee's tone sincere/empathetic/professional?   Y / N / NA
10. Did the employee add to your service experience?   Y / N / NA
11. Did you feel valued as a customer?   Y / N / NA
12. Would you recommend this employee for hire to your business? Y / N / NA

Overall, rate your satisfaction with this employee

     1   2   3   4   5   6   7   8   9   10
    YUCK   EH, OK   WOW

Notes/Comments:

B. Set a goal for three to five contacts per week in which you will use your Mystery Shop form to evaluate the service of others. If you primarily deal with customers by telephone, then shop those types of businesses. It is helpful to pick businesses that may be in a similar business or in direct competition with yours.

Be prepared to talk about your interactions at your next team meeting. Rotate the mystery shopper among all team members, or have all participate and randomly pick those to "story tell" about their experience. Don't forget to relate the lessons learned for the improvement of your own service.

C. Among your team members, complete the following:
If there is one thing I'd like to see the company improve on, it would be:

A final comment on customer surveys. If you decide to use written questionnaires or comment cards of any kind, be sure to have postage paid. I'm continually amazed at the survey cards I come across that do not have postage provided. And these are from large, they-should-know-better companies. It is a rule not to be broken: if you want feedback, make it easy for your customers to give it. Enough said on that!

B = Believe What They Are Telling You

Why wouldn't we believe our customers? We have taken the time to ask for their opinions, of course we'll listen to what they say.

This is where denial kicks in. As a loyal and committed employee, we often find it hard to take criticism about our businesses. We either don't really listen to what the customers are telling us, or just as bad, we begin to justify our position and place blame elsewhere. Imagine for a moment that you are in a manufacturing plant that supplies plastic products for the auto industry. You have just conducted a customer satisfaction survey and learned that your customers are receiving an abnormally high number of shipments with cracked plastic parts.

Your response: "Well, they left here just fine, what are THEY doing with them once the parts arrive?" Or, "They were OK when we loaded them on the truck. I wouldn't doubt that they were damaged in shipment. I've seen how those truck drivers handle them. The customer just needs to file an insurance claim." And the worst of all, "Something must be happening at the buyer's warehouse. They were fine when they left our factory." In any case, the customer has not been helped. It's a poor way of basically saying, "We've done our job—it's in your hands now." What a shame. This type of thinking and rationalizing will soon lead to customer defection. It is a narrow way of viewing the customer experience. The customer's experience begins when you or your company are first contacted, and it extends right through until the product is in use and has been paid for. In fact, the experience really goes beyond that to include service after the sale, advertising reinforcement, warranties, and right on until the next purchase is made. It's a complete cycle that theoretically should not be broken by lack of attention to a problem.

Recently I worked with a retailer that was in a similar sort of denial as to their role. Different circumstances, but the same excusing of the issues. This store was very diligent about seeking customer feedback. Historically, they had done quite well in their service measurements, but an undesirable trend began with the decline in the perceptions of the frontline staff. Reports were coming back monthly showing that the sales and service staffs were no longer being perceived as "helpful, friendly, or even professional." The retailer remarked, "Well, that's not altogether surprising with the unemployment ratios we're facing in this area. Heck, we're lucky just to have warm bodies that can take the money and provide the correct change." Is that not outrageous! No wonder the store was getting feedback like this on its surveys. Instead of investing in the training and motivation, instead of reviewing how the recruitment and retention practices are being revamped in light of the low unemployment, this store was just excusing the problem. This is a very dangerous trap to fall into.

Here are some other common phrases heard that should sound the alarms:

★ "This is not a good measurement of overall satisfaction anyway. We all know that only the disgruntled customers take time to complete the surveys."

★ "I'm not so sure this isn't just a fluke in the reporting this month. Let's wait until next month's report to see what it says."

★ "I've never trusted these reports anyway. The way the questions are phrased, it invites complaints."

★ "What do these customers expect anyway. Nobody is going to make these guys happy."

The point not to be missed here is that no matter the issue, if it's affecting the overall customer care it shouldn't be passed off with excuses. And whether you are part of management or a member of the all-important frontline, you can have an impact on the situation. But nothing will happen if you don't believe the results in the first place.

C = Communicate Your Results

Too often, organizations gather this type of customer feedback, and then they fail to share it. It gets hidden away in some management closet. Well little use it serves there. This type of information needs to be shared, and shared creatively!

Not every audience is appropriate for the information gathered, but you should go through a checklist of who could benefit from the information. Take, for example, some very positive results from either a quantitative or qualitative survey. Think how this could be built into your client communications (newsletters, report letters, brochure materials, Web site, shopping bags, etc.). Imagine how powerful it could be as part of your recruitment and training materials for Human Resources. Just imagine that you are interviewing for a position at a new company and they roll out some incredibly strong customer satisfaction statistics, or maybe some testimonial quotes from customers. Don't you feel better about the company and your potential for enjoying the work there? Strong positive endorsements can serve as wonderful reinforcement messages that current clients are making a good decision. Likewise, they are effective morale boosters for staff in all departments. Use the information at team meetings, company meetings, and special event gatherings. Some companies have even printed great results of testimonials on T-shirts, coffee mugs, and other specialty items.

So it's fun to think of ways to use the good comments, but what about the not so good? These need to be shared as well, but with a little more caution and tact. Customers want to know that they've been heard. Individual letters back to disgruntled customers can be very effective. Thank them for their input; you have no way of improving without it. It lets them know that you are listening, and that you have plans to address the situation. Customers will tend to have more faith in your commitment to turn things around when you are honest in sharing deficiencies.

At Ben & Jerry's ice cream company, they have incredibly effective letters to customers (you'll enjoy this story). A customer who was seven months pregnant had a midnight craving for Chunky Monkey ice cream. She managed to persuade her husband to brave a blinding snowstorm for a pint. Upon scooping the ice cream into a bowl, she was most disappointed at the sparseness of walnuts in the product. She was accustomed to many more from past experience. She wrote the company and complained. The letter responding to her situation was great! First, the company apologized to her for the "wimpy, anemic, under-chunked pint." What's more, they included a coupon for a free pint because, as the letter stated, "you have to feed that baby." Score! They just created a customer experience.

D = Do Something with What You've Learned

Sounds like a kindergarten message, doesn't it? It is fairly basic, but it is so often dropped. It's a matter of priorities, so make sure that delivering the customer experience is one of your priorities. This doesn't mean that you have to address every issue ever raised by a customer. You are encouraged, however, to sort out the priority problem areas and begin a plan of attack. Your time, energy, and, yes, sometimes money, are investments that will reap great rewards.

Notes

Note to team leader: In many instances the responsibility to do something regarding poor customer responses is a management issue. If left in the hands of the frontline, they'd surely take action. It may be because management is more removed from the customer that they traditionally don't act as quickly. They don't see the pain as clearly. Think about it. How can you make sure that action is taken where appropriate?

It's a Wrap

Did you catch all of the following points?

Feedback: Ask and you shall receive!
- ★ Some conventional and unconventional methods
  - • Surveys
  - • Hotline
  - • Follow-up letters
  - • Employees listen for comments
- ★ Don't forget to survey lost customers
- ★ Quantitative versus qualitative methods

Feedback: Believe what they are telling you
- ★ Don't dismiss criticism
- ★ Don't place blame elsewhere
- ★ Do listen for phrases that sound the "defensive alarm"

Feedback: Communicate your results
- ★ Share the data—good and bad
- ★ Make it fun!

Feedback: Do something with what you've learned

Technology and E-Commerce: Enhancer or Inhibitor

It is very dangerous in today's world to write about topics such as technology and e-commerce. Why? At the rate that these areas are advancing, the information we give you may well be out-of-date by the time our words meet the press. On the other hand, that's actually one of the beauties of technology. It can be exciting, scary, complex, rapid, confusing, simplifying, and (to most of us) a complete mystery all at once. It makes for dreams come true, and it's been known to make nightmares a reality.

As we discuss technology and e-commerce, we want you to look beyond the gadget-of-the-day and look at technology's impact from the

BULLSEYE

WELCOME TO *%SQUSSHH*%SQUAWK, MAY I *%SQUSSHH *%SQUAWK ORDER?

YES, I'D LIKE 3 KIDZ PAKS WITH MILK, 1 CHICKEN SANDWICH WITH NO MAYO, AND 1 CHOMPER BURGER WITH CHEESE.

THAT'LL BE *%SQUSSHH*%SQUAWK, PLEASE DRIVE AROU*%SQUSSHH!

McNAIR/NATION

SO, KIDS, HOW'S YOUR *%SQUSSHH*%SQUAWK?

perspective of the customer. Quite simply, how is technology enhancing or inhibiting the customer experience?

I was reading a copy of *Down East* (the magazine of the state of Maine) when I came across a wonderful note from one of their readers:

> "I believe many people desperately want to retain a simple world, a caring world, and whether we are crazy or bitter or reckless or moody, or are born an outsider, we are all seeking the great gift of contentment, the one perfect, never-to-be forgotten gift that I doubt will ever be bestowed by a computer."

Can't you identify with this? Don't get me wrong—I have my own love-hate relationship with my computer, voice mail, e-mail, faxes, DirectTV, Web sites, ATMs, cellphones, scanners, digital cameras, security systems, pagers, and the innumerable trappings of our sophisticated/automated/electronically translated world. There are days when I covet my hardware and software niceties, and then there are those other times. Fact is, technological advancements are here to stay, and it's our challenge to make human use of them.

Being There, Electronically of Course

While watching a morning news show recently, I was struck by a story of an innovative company and their use of the Internet. Before talking about their product, let's first describe the customer and her need.

The need: You are the parent of an 11-month-old little girl. She is your first child. Being a working mother is no cakewalk. Each day you drop off your child at the day care and drive to work with a blanket of guilt. And when guilt is not there, then sadness takes its place. You miss seeing your little girl at play, watching her toddle, watching her sleep. And forbid that you have any concerns for the quality of the care she'll be receiving. Day in and day out, you somehow deal with it.

The solution: a Web site "see you" cam. For a rather small fee you can access the Web, enter your pass code, and have instant access to a live video telecast from your child's day care. Wow! While it will never replace being there, what a miracle of technology. And on the newscast—parents, day care workers, even employers—all were interviewed for their reactions to this creative application of technology. Unanimously, and with sincere conviction, each person interviewed spoke of the benefits—the comfort, the security, and all the tangibles and intangibles of such a service. It is truly a win-win situation!

Imagine the uses of this same Web video service in hospitals, nursing homes, and home health agencies. Does it have its downsides and its detractors? Sure it does. Regardless of the pros and cons, however, it is still a great example of a creative use of technology to enhance customer service.

One of the more creative and human uses of technology that we've seen is by Jansport, a leading manufacturer of outdoor supplies such as the ever-popular backpack. Not only do we love this company for their quality products and their lifetime guarantees, but most of all because they have a personal service culture. Let me explain what I mean by personal service culture. The 11-year-old son of a friend of mine has had one of their backpacks for years. It's been battered about in lockers, lunchrooms, sand, surf, and sludge. As life took its toll, the zipper finally broke. In a mailer (provided by the company) the young man's father sent off this well-worn backpack to be repaired—at no charge I might add. Within a week he received the following postcard in the mail—addressed directly to his son:

Hi!

It's me, your favorite Back Pack. Warranty Service Camp is really cool. The other packs are really different, and I love my pack counselor. I miss hanging out with you and carrying your gear all the time. I can't wait to see you. They say they're sending me home soon. Gotta run . . . we're doing zipper races today.

Little Pack

P.S. If you need to reach me, my numbers are on the other side of this card.

Consider what Jansport has just done. In a very personal, human-touch way, they have used technology to communicate their service while building a heck of a bond with the customer. They knew the pack's owner by name. I'm sure their database tells them how long he's had the pack, how old he is, and most likely what some of his interests are. After all, they could have just sent a card that said they had received the product and it was due for return by XX date. Many companies don't even bother with that level of communication. But Jansport chose to innovatively apply their technology to provide a personal level of service. And they didn't stop there. When the backpack was returned, it had another postcard enclosed.

Hi,

I'm your pack's counselor, Big J. S. We really enjoyed getting to know little J. S. at Warranty Service Camp this year—what a star! A strapping little rascal, your pack led the pack in bug smashing, carrying ghost stories, and as you know, Little J. S. made quite a showing in the zipper races.

We know you must have missed the little bagger like crazy. You'll be pleased to know that we worked out those little problems that you told us about, so your pack is back to full zip strength.

Every happiness,

Big J. S.

Obviously, these notes were computer generated. And note the language: "zipper races, zip strength" and all the references to backpacks. They must have countless form letters in their database that tailor the note to the receiver. It certainly shows that they know the product, the problem, the customer, and how to serve!

A Walk on the Uglier Side

Contrast this with a call I made recently to my laptop computer manufacturer's help line. After what seemed to be an endless journey through their Web site, a fruitless effort to pinpoint my specific problem, I finally abandoned the Web and sought the comfort of the 24-hour help line at 12:30 A.M. As expected, I was connected directly into an automated phone system. For my appetizer, I was presented with four choices of buttons to push. My entree menu included no less than eight alternatives. My dessert was another six, and my fourth menu—oh, I don't even recall. Finally, for the first time apparent to me, I could actually push 0 for a real live person. I had now been on the phone for almost 20 minutes when Tom answered and attempted to clarify that I am with the U.S. military. "No," I told him, at which point he stated that he couldn't help me, and I must call back for their residential customer service. "Please, NO!," I implored, not wanting to go through their automated maze again. Unfortunately, I had no other option. Tom couldn't access my records, nor could he transfer me to the correct department. At least that was his claim. As the clock ticked towards 2 A.M., I abandoned the call and slumped off to bed. How I longed to just call and reach a friendly person who empathized with my need and could assure me of a solution. Strike three, I was out.

Here's one more great story from the dark side of technology. In a letter to syndicated newspaper columnist Ann Landers, a poor "customer" related being hounded by the billing department of the local department of education about a student loan. The wacky thing was that the billing department admitted that the correct loan balance was $0.00. The problem was that the computer had no way of deleting this balance from its accounts receivable without receiving a check. In order to stop the harassment of monthly collection letters, this dutiful customer sent in a check for $0. She found that calling the customer service center was useless because "they don't always communicate with the billing department." Happy ending? The collection efforts did stop, but the craziest thing of all was that the billing department did try to cash the $0 check!

And guess who gets to deal with the customer now? You! You get the "recovery" of this customer who feels abused by your not-so-friendly technology and service policies. That's why the hands-on skills of empathy, listening, rapport building, and dealing with the challenging customers are so crucial to your success.

Unfortunately, the above situations are becoming quite the norm. Ever tally how many calls you make to businesses in a day that are actually answered by a live person within five (we think that's reasonable) rings. If you track it for a while, you will find that percentage to be pretty low. In fact, let's do that.

Allow 15 minutes to complete the following table.

Exercise

EXERCISE: PERSON TO PERSON

Select five places of business to call. They could be your competition, one of your suppliers, or just a pick from the telephone directory. Note how the call was received and any comments you may have. Share these with your service team and discuss how people perceive calls into your business or department.

NAME/TYPE OF BUSINESS	# RINGS	L = LIVE P = IN PERSON	COMMENTS

It Can Be the Simple Things, Even with Technology

Sometimes the word *technology* is too grandiose a word for many of us. It conjures up images of satellite transmissions, bytes, and strange programmer types to make it all work. What's silly is that most of us don't take advantage of the simplest offerings of today's technology—offerings that truly benefit the customer.

It's hard to imagine that at one point or another you haven't called Pizza Hut for a home delivery. What's the first thing they ask you? Your home phone number. Give them that and they may soon say, "Oh Miss Jones, would you like the same pizza you ordered last time? A large, thin crust pepperoni and mushroom?" It's become second nature to many of us now, but do you remember how impressed you were the first time it happened? They not only knew your last order, they knew how to find your house—the directions you used to repeat each time were now in their system. So what else might they know about you? I'll give you a hint: don't ask them how much you spent on pizza in the last year. They can tell you that too, and you don't want to know. What's important is that they know. How many other businesses that you deal with do you wish kept those kind of records?

Here's another example of a simple phone system helper. If you call Great American Business Products out of Houston, Texas, it's unlikely that you will actually be placed on hold. Their statistics show they answer calls within an average of 20 seconds. Should you have to hold, on one of those inevitable busy days, then you will hear a quite unusual recording. The message says, "Because you're on hold, we want to give you a bonus item for holding. When the representative comes on the line, please ask what your bonus item will be." A free gift—don't get that much, do you? As you might imagine, Great American Business Products sells office supply items. So you might get a free box of pens or notepads. Nonetheless, this small gesture catches the callers' attention and lets them know that they are valued.

When I think of large call centers, I also appreciate the occasional ones that give me an estimate of how long I can expect to be on hold. Kind of funny, isn't it? Don't get the impression that I like to hold! But as customers, we have become so accustomed to holding that by telling us how long we can expect to hold we are somehow grateful. You see, it allows us the option to continue holding or to call back later. It puts a little bit of control into our hands. For example, when I'm in the office, I often choose to put a call on the speakerphone, and I continue working while waiting for a representative. Furthermore, most call centers have peak hours. I appreciate the hold message telling me hours that are more accessible. I may not always have the choice to call at another time, but if I do it's my option.

So how is your phone answered at work? Has your business, like so many, gone to highly automated voice systems? Is the system customer friendly? What messages do you have for people on hold? Once the customer is on the line, how much information do you already know about them and their history with your company? Do you use the information that you have readily available to reinforce your relationship with the customer? So much can be done in this simple area, yet so many ignore the potential.

E-commerce and E-service— They Can Be One in the Same

We're surrounded. If you're not already part of the e-world, it's time to wave the white flag. Whether it's a print advertisement or on TV or the radio, you rarely see one that doesn't end with something.com. It's an instant access, 24-hour, 7-day a week way to do business. Who wouldn't jump at it? Isn't that a large part of the service equation, not to mention the worldwide exposure that e-commerce provides from a sales and marketing perspective?

Let's look at some statistics. In a comprehensive 1999 study conducted by Cisco Systems and the University of Texas, it was revealed that the U.S. Internet economy exceeded all previous estimates, producing over $300 billion in annual revenues and more than two million jobs by the end of 1998. The same study projected the economic impact by the end of 1999 to be $507 million (and that projection came true!). These figures include not only actual Internet commerce, but revenue and jobs associated with infrastructure and applications software.

In another survey done by Sage Software, Inc., 70 percent of small businesses surveyed have a corporate Web site or one under construction. Of those companies that didn't, 65 percent said they planned to have a site in the future.

And while we're at it, let's consider some statistics from the customer's side of things. Households with at least one personal computer have grown from 40 to 60 percent in less than three years. With ever declining prices and simplified offerings for home computers, you can expect this won't be slowing. With almost a quarter of a billion Internet users as of the writing of this book, there are projected to be more than 500 million people surfing by 2003.

The impacts to our lives as consumers—and to our lives as business professionals—are limited only by our vision of what could be. Imagine some of the conveniences that technology could offer (some may even be reality by the time you read this!):

★ Your handheld computer is tracking the satellite positioning of your child's school bus so you know exactly where it is and when to expect its arrival.

★ Better yet, this same unit is tracking the whereabouts of your teenager as he drives your new car. You can know the exact locations he visited, the speed he traveled, and just when he'll walk through your door (after curfew, of course).

★ Your cellular telephone "talks to" a vending machine, allowing you to purchase a soda, stamps, or a newspaper without paying cash. Known as m-commerce, technology is available that allows you to shop and pay bills using your cell phone.

★ As you head for an appointment, don't worry about traffic delays. No waiting for the report from *SkyChopper II*. You'll have real-time access to all road conditions for your route. Some automobile manufacturers are now offering as an option navigational consoles that provide maps and specific directions at the push of a button (Keep your eyes on the road!).

★ Grocery shopping—who has time? Your refrigerator will scan all contents and send electronic orders to your food/supply distribution center for delivery. Furthermore, this smart fridge will suggest recipes that can be made with the contents available.

★ You are paying all your bills electronically. Your home and business mailboxes are no longer cluttered with all that unnecessary paper as invoices will come electronically as well.

★ Airlines will send a real-time notification to your pager or computer if a flight is running late. They will even tell you about traffic delays coming into or from your designated airport.

★ Think of the fun at family reunions. No more missed relatives due to lengthy travel. Keep in touch with Web cams, the Polaroid of tomorrow.

We could go on, but this chapter is not trying to instill fear (or excitement as the case may be) for where our world of communications is heading. Our purpose is to get you thinking creatively about how your business can be impacted, internally and externally, by this e-world.

I especially like what one company has done. It's a magazine called *Fast Company*. At *Fast Company*, you may be reading an article that you particularly like. You immediately think of a friend or work associate who would enjoy the article as well. Here's what you do. You don't have to tear your article out and make a trip to the copy machine. Simply go to the *Fast Company* Web site, pull up that issue, and go the article that you want to send. There's an icon that says "Send this page to a friend." You simply enter the friend's e-mail address along with a personal message. Isn't that great! And think of the benefit to *Fast Company*. They now have the e-mail address of a potential new reader, and chances are this person may be interested in a subscription. It's another win-win! I wish every magazine had this option. I'd be forwarding articles all day long.

Another creative use of a Web site may not have come into its own yet, but watch out! It's called computer telephony. It's relatively inexpensive software that allows talking over the Internet. This has such potential because it brings a personalization and humanization into the Web site world. It's a helping hand for the "I'm lost in your Web site" customer, and it provides an opportunity for helping those with more specialized needs that aren't often accommodated in general Web browsing. Many home and office computers don't yet have the power and software to conduct business this way, but it will be a standard soon.

We are seeing more and more touch screens in retail and travel-related businesses. It's great for hospitals, libraries, museums, and certain restaurants. Heck, Disney World has had touch screens in its park for years. Ever watch the way children surround them? So in getting to the point, do your products have options that the customers might like to customize? How could this type of technology benefit your clientele? How might it benefit you as well?

As a natural step from touch screens, we are once again led to Web technology. Lands' End capitalized on this with the creation of your "Personal Model." This feature allows women to input their personal dimensions into the site, and a model is created for them that can then try on clothes. Haven't we all seen something that looked good on the rack that didn't have quite the same appeal on the body. Well this is a start. And taking this one step further, a company in London has created a camera booth that takes your picture from numerous angles to create a computer-transferable image for you. This photographic cloning allows you to put yourself into the World Wide Web as a virtual customer extraordinaire. Could shopping get any more fun?

Whether it's retail, entertainment, health care, real estate, or politics, almost every industry is learning how to take advantage of a fuller customer experience through the Internet. This is one area where you don't want to be caught behind the eight ball. Check out what your competition is doing, and see if you can one-up them with technology.

Protecting and Projecting Your E-mage

With the Internet's foray into today's business operations, Web sites started sprouting like weeds. Too often these Web sites were flat in function and awkward in appearance. Don't forget, the first entrances into Web sites were designed by techie people, people who often didn't focus on the service elements. Many of these early sites were (and are) nothing but electronic brochures for an organization. Flat Web sites are not interactive, not communicative, and often not even up-to-date. They don't invite a customer in, and they don't engage them once online. For a Web site to be effective, it should be one of many extensions of your business. It should have the look, feel, and quality image that are consistent with your organization. It should offer easy, direct access for customers to ask questions as well as give comments. Here are some general considerations for you to e-valuate:

★ Does your Web site design reflect your image? Is it busy or clean? Is it colorful, trendy, and techie, or warm, soft, and understated?

★ Can browsers easily contact you? Do you have proper response support?

★ Is your site updated regularly? Does it have opportunities for the customer to interact?

★ Do you ask the customer questions about their perceptions/satisfaction with the services or products you offer?

★ Do you have customer chat rooms where instant dialogue can take place with your organization or other customers?

★ How quickly are e-mail inquiries responded to?

★ Do you send e-mails to confirm an order, as well as when it's been shipped?

★ Do you ask the customers about their hobbies, interests, birthdays, or any other key profile-type questions?

★ Do you help direct them to related sites, offer repair advice, or creative uses of your products?

★ Do you assure them of security and site integrity when information is being gathered?

Allow 15 minutes to complete the following tables.

EXERCISE: E-MAGINE THE POSSIBILITIES

As a team, brainstorm ideas that could most improve your phone system and/or your Web site. Try to name at least 6 to 10 ideas. Take a vote and rank them in order of your top three suggestions.

Exercise

Improving Service Through Technology Suggestions

1.

2.

3.

Don't just let these ideas collect dust. Take a stab at doing two things with this information. First, take the initiative to start researching what resources would be needed to implement the above ideas. Try and come up with some basic cost estimates and identify who is needed to assist with implementation. Secondly, submit this information to your management with your thoughts on why these technology enhancements would benefit the customers and/or the organization.

Don't Let Your Technology Byte You

A common mistake businesses make is to upgrade technology without providing the support behind it. It's much like building a beautiful home without adding the wiring or plumbing—the things that allow the structure to function as a home. By support we are talking about the training, the staffing, and whatever components are necessary to make best use of the respective technology. To think of it in the simplest of terms, it would be comparable to a bank opening a new ATM site that is always out of money. You must not forget that when a service is offered, customers expect it to work.

One thing is certain about our tech-based customers—they can walk even faster off a Web site than out of your door. Their access to the competition is just a click away. No more parking headaches or time invested in the drive to your business. Imagine the loyalty it takes to keep the customer from simply clicking you to oblivion! True market leaders know that the total customer experience is what will differentiate their product or service from all the rest in today's highly competitive world.

Remember that current and emerging technology, no matter how fast, sophisticated, accurate, or cost-efficient, is still dependent on people for its success. The term "high-tech, high touch" really does apply to the world of customer care today and in the future. Your challenge is to utilize technology to enhance service levels, not to let it inhibit giving exceptional customer service.

It's a Wrap

Did you catch all of the following points?

Some creative uses of technology in customer service

Some not-so-creative applications of technology

Use of technology doesn't have to be "rocket science"
★ *Pizza Hut*—recording customer preferences
★ *Great American Business Products*—"hold for your free gift"
★ "Your estimated hold time is"

E-commerce and e-service—one and the same?
★ Internet usage is exploding—500 million by 2003!
★ E-business is Big Business—$500 billion at end of 1999
★ E-magine these possibilities
   • Track your child/teenager by computer
   • The refrigerator that refills itself
   • Shop and pay bills using your cell phone
   • Computer telephony—talking over the Internet
★ Is your Web site customer friendly? Some tips.

CHAPTER TWELVE

Lights, Camera, Action: Service Stars

Most of you reading this book share at least one thing in common. You are not only service providers, you are service receivers. You come in contact with literally thousands upon thousands of customer service providers. In fact, I can think of no profession (and customer service is a profession) for which we should be better prepared through personal experience to do a great job.

Let's face it, we have seen it all: rude, indifferent, and exceptional care. We know what kind of service we like as well as the service that drives us crazy. Think of your personal experiences as a customer over the past week. Think of the best experience you had with a service provider. Why was the experience special? My experience occurred

upon arriving home from vacation. I had spent a relaxing week in Los Angeles visiting family and returned home on a late evening flight. Since I was to be gone for 10 days, I had decided not to leave my car at the airport and to take a taxi home. Upon arriving at 11:00 P.M. and getting my bags, I was assigned to a cab (actually a van) driven by Maurice. I was tired after the long flight. I'm sure Maurice was as well. Nonetheless, it's always good to be back home, and I was anxious to catch up on what had been going on at home while I was away. I was in luck! Maurice was friendly, talkative (not rambling), and genuinely anxious to engage in small talk. Since I'm fortunate to live in a city that thrives on tourism, Maurice spends most of his time transporting visitors from the airport to downtown hotels. He quickly picked up on the fact that I was a local, and filled me in on how the weather had been, events going on in the city, and even the latest on local political races in progress (OK, he did slip in some of his political views). Had I been a tourist, I'm sure he was prepared with restaurant recommendations, sightseeing tips, and other useful information. When he dropped me off at home after midnight, he noticed that another passenger had left a bag in the backseat of the van. Remembering the passenger's address from the earlier drop-off, Maurice said, "Guess I'll stop by and deliver this bag on my way home. Mr. Jones (he remembered the passenger's name!) will need it in the morning." Now, Maurice may never be mayor or president of the chamber of commerce, but I can think of no one better suited to represent his city than Maurice.

Maurice, you see, is a customer Service Star. There are hundreds of thousands of stars out there, but we need millions more! All of us can be stars. There are some very specific things we can do that will help us become a Service Star. And we can help our team be viewed as a real service-oriented team that stands out from other organizations and other businesses. Those attributes of Service Stars are the subject of this final capstone chapter.

Let's first look at Service Stars. You all have them in your organizations. What they have in common is an intense desire to exceed the customer's expectations. They want their customers to walk away dazzled. Stars give everyone else goals to shoot for and a benchmark to be measured against. It's important to remember that everyone can become a star just by taking on the challenge of being exceptional. So let's talk about the characteristics of a Service Star.

Characteristics of a Service Star

★ Motivation
★ Flexibility
★ Energy and enthusiasm
★ Ownership

Motivated to Serve

If there is one attribute that all Service Stars share, it is motivation—actually a passion—to serve and help others. Stars realize great personal satisfaction and reward from serving. They feel a genuine (and that word is important) need, want, and desire to help others.

Here's what motivation looks like! Mario is an assistant general manager in one of the restaurants at the Pierre Hotel in New York City. In New York, as well as most other large cities, just getting to work in the morning can be a major hassle. Every day, Mario commutes to work, and that's enough to start anyone's day off on a low note. Well, Mario loves his job. He says that when he arrives at the restaurant and starts seeing the list of who's coming in for the day, and who they will be serving at this five-star hotel and restaurant (notice they rate the hotels by number of stars), it's like caffeine starting to surge through him. He immediately gets excited about the day and getting ready to serve people. Mario is sincerely motivated to serve.

Flexible

In Chapter 9 we talked about all the different customers you have to deal with on a day-to-day basis, including the challenging ones. Flexibility is the key to being able to maneuver through all the craziness, all the customer demands, and all the challenges that get thrown at you each and every day. Customer Service Stars seem to be able to rise above negative situations and adapt their behavior based on the events going on around them.

Former *Good Morning America* co-anchor Joan Lunden had this to say in an interview shortly after learning she was to be replaced on the show. She said, "I can admit to feeling scared and vulnerable sometimes. But then I talk to myself and about how I *choose* to look at things. When life tosses you a curve ball, you can get mad, and say, 'Why did this happen to me?' or, 'Cool. Wonder if I can catch that ball.'" That's flexibility. We sometimes refer to it as making lemonade out of lemons. Service Stars know that recipe well and are flexible and adaptive enough to make gallons of lemonade every day on the frontlines of service.

Energy and Enthusiasm

Think about people you like to be around. They may be family members, friends, coworkers, or customers. No matter who they are, they are just plain fun to be around. They seem to radiate energy and enthusiasm. If you are having a bad day or are down in the dumps, just being around these people gives you a shot in the arm, a positive jolt. Imagine the impact you could have on your customers by radiating energy and enthusiasm—by infecting them with your sincere personality. Put another way, if you don't have energy and enthusiasm, change your mind and get it!

Ownership

Have you ever dealt with someone in an organization and come away feeling like you just talked to the president instead of a frontline associate? Have you ever said to yourself following a customer service interaction, "Gosh, I was lucky to get that person. I hope to get him or her again." Or have you walked away from a situation saying, "Wow! I can't believe they were able to do that for me." If you answered yes to these questions, you were lucky enough to be dealing with a real-life Service Star!

Service Stars take ownership of customers, situations, and problems. They use every bit of the power and authority they have been given by management. They make you feel like you are the only customer they have helped all day, even though they may have seen hundreds before you. Empowerment is a word that's a bit overused in this country. We have everything from empowerment zones to empowered employees to empowered work teams, and on and on. While the word does get quite a workout, the meaning behind it is very powerful, especially as it relates to customer care. Stars really take the power that they have been given to serve customers and to take ownership of their problems. In fact, true Service Stars find ways to help customers even when the letter of the law or policy prevents it.

Late one evening at a nursing home in the Chicago area, a senior manager discovered what taking ownership means. While taking a break, she decided to walk the floors a little to get some exercise. She encountered a young college student who worked part-time cleaning floors and doing other custodial tasks. Noticing how quiet it was that late at night, she told the young man that it would be fine if he brought in a Walkman and listened to music to break the silence a little. Without hesitating, the young man replied, "Oh no, I couldn't do that. If one of the residents cried out or needed something, I wouldn't hear them." Talk about ownership! Here's a college student on a part-time job cleaning floors at night and he feels ownership for the care of the patients. Is he a Service Star? You bet.

Great Service Is HABITual

Let's look at Service Stardom through a slightly different lens. What daily habits can we engage in to help keep us motivated, energetic, enthusiastic, flexible, and empowered? These characteristics are states of mind. It's one thing to get up in the morning, look in the mirror, and say, "I think I'll be motivated at work today." It's another thing to follow through. Remember, exceptional customer service requires behavior modification. That means changing habits, practicing new techniques, and undoing some old ones. Here are a few for your consideration.

BE CONSISTENT

Service Stars are consistent in how they deliver service. Have you ever purchased a new car? The day you first go to the dealership to look at cars the sales associate couldn't be nicer, more accommodating, willing to move heaven and earth to ensure you find just the automobile you want at a price you can afford. He's your best friend for that period of time. A week after you buy the car something minor needs adjusting, so you call the dealership. "Bill who? Oh yeah, why don't you call the service department and make an appointment to bring it in?" says the sales associate. I have no quarrel with having to call and schedule the car for service. I realize that the associate who sold me the car isn't the person who can fix it. It's just that I would like to feel a little of the charm, care, and concern that I experienced when I purchased the car carry over to at least my first service experience.

Contrast that with the philosophy of Men's Wearhouse, a popular retail clothing chain, where each customer is viewed as a lifetime customer. When patrons return to pick up an altered suit or trousers, associates go out of their way to treat them as well, or even better, than they did when they sold them the clothing. Service Stars have a way of making you feel special even after they have closed the deal.

BE CREATIVE

There's a furniture store in Boston owned by two of the most creative and customer-oriented gentlemen we've met. These guys are not only Service Stars, they are borderline goofballs. They do all of their own television commercials (they are hilarious) and genuinely want to make furniture shopping fun. Here's where creativity comes in. These owners figured out that many customers bring small children with them. They also figured out that adults will stay longer and shop more seriously if the kids are happy. So they constructed a large children's play area inside the store with every type of game imaginable. By the way, you have to walk all the way through the store to get to the playground, so mom and dad can see the furniture before settling down to serious shopping. The kids are happy, so the parents are happy. It's simple. And one more thing. When you leave their store, your car windows have been washed! It's no wonder that this store has the highest sales of any furniture outlet in the Boston area.

Creativity pays off both in terms of service and profitability. At a paper processing facility in eastern Tennessee, the associates in the shipping department had a group picture made of themselves. Every time a shipment of huge rolls of paper goes out, the people who prepared it for shipment circle their faces on the picture, sign their names, and enclose the picture with the shipment. What a creative way to take ownership and personalize an impersonal process like shipping paper!

LOVE WHAT YOU DO

Job Factors as Rated by Employees*

1. Appreciation of their work

2. Feeling "in"

3. Help with personal problems

4. Security

5. Wages

6. Interesting work

7. Growth potential

8. Personal loyalty

9. Working conditions

*As reported by The Public Institute, 1999.

In almost every survey of the factors that motivate employees in the workplace, job satisfaction is at or near the top of the list, far surpassing pay and benefits. Service Stars, however, are far more than satisfied with their job, they love what they do. If you have a frontline service job, the plain fact of the matter is you'd better love serving customers because you will be doing it eight or more hours a day. And customers can see straight through you and tell whether you enjoy your work.

I recently met a customer care associate who loves serving her customers. She works as a branch office administrator for Edward Jones, an international brokerage firm. Her office is in Daytona Beach, Florida. During the fires that damaged Florida from Jacksonville to Orlando, she went through her client list and made phone calls to customers who lived in the fire area simply to say, "How are you doing? Things okay? Do you need anything? Can we offer you a ride anywhere? Do you need some bottled water? Can we bring bottles to your house?" That only comes from somebody who loves her customers.

PAY ATTENTION TO THE DETAILS

There's a popular phrase, "Don't sweat the small stuff." While this might be good advice in dealing with stress in our personal lives, the phrase doesn't really apply in customer care. To customers, some more than others, everything is big stuff. If I work in a hospital and order flat sheets, I don't want to receive fitted sheets from the vendor. If I'm really particular about what kind of rental car I drive, I am concerned about that detail when I show up at the airport desk to claim my reserved car. Service Stars are very attentive to detail and go to great lengths to ensure that every need of their customer, however small, is met.

Nordstrom is well known in the retailing world for being great on customer service. They started out many years ago as only a shoe store. A practice they have continued through the years as they grew larger is that of measuring feet. The first time a customer comes in, they measure her feet. Not just one but both! When's the last time you had your feet measured prior to buying a pair of shoes? Just another detail that Star organizations attend to.

LOVE CHANGE, CHAOS, AND SURPRISE

It's been said often that the only constant in life is change. The world around us is changing so fast—technology, specific customer likes and dislikes, or the attitudes of society in general—that it hardly seems we have much choice but to embrace change. Service Stars thrive on change and the excitement and new opportunities that change creates.

RECHARGE YOURSELF

We talked about this earlier but it bears repeating. It is a rare individual who can stay motivated, energetic, and enthusiastic eight or more hours a day. We all need a break. Service Stars know when the stress, frustration, and workload is starting to get to them and that they need to take a break, to get offstage for a few minutes. These same individuals strive to maintain balance in their lives between work, family, and leisure activities.

Rate Your Service Star Habits

Which of the habits of Service Stars are you good at? Which do you need to improve on? Give yourself a grade from A (I'm a star at this) to F (I'm totally lacking in this habit).

Grade

Be consistent _____

Be creative _____

Love what you do _____

Pay attention to the details _____

Love change, chaos, and surprise _____

Recharge yourself _____

Building Career Paths Through Customer Care

Another characteristic of many Service Stars is an intense desire to be the best in their field, to really excel in the profession of customer care. They know they are good at what they do and that they have excellent people skills. Perhaps they want to lead their customer service team or serve as a coach or a mentor to new associates.

With the growing trend in this country toward flatter organization structures, lateral moves and job shifts are becoming much more common. More than ever before, your ability to advance in the organization will be based on the value you add and the value you are able to create for your customers. According to the national executive recruiting firm, Korn-Ferry, "In the new millennium, people who will be rising to the senior ranks as presidents and CEOs will be those who understand customer value more so than at any time in the past."

How do put yourself in the position to be recognized as someone who can take advantage of opportunities to move up in the organization? Here are some suggestions:

BETTER . . . BEST

Ever heard the phrase, "If you always do what you've always done, you'll always get what you always got?" Translated into the language of customer care, this means simply that what might be exceptional service today will in all probability be just satisfactory service tomorrow. The bar is constantly being raised. Service Stars, in particular team leaders and coaches, are constantly asking the question, "How can I be 1 percent better at providing exceptional customer service today than I was yesterday?" Notice, I said 1 percent. Doesn't seem like much, but small, incremental improvements on a frequent basis are easier to achieve than large, breakthrough improvements. The now commonplace automated teller machine was a breakthrough service improvement in the financial services industry when it was invented in the 1960s. Since that time, numerous incremental improvements have been made in ATM technology, including range of services, accessibility, and security. Continuous improvement may come in attitude, communication, technology, or any of the areas we have discussed in this book. The important thing is constant improvement.

In his book, *Escape from the Box: The Wonder of Human Potential*, retired Air Force Colonel Edward Hubbard recounts his six and one-half years as a prisoner of war during the Vietnam War. Hubbard reflects on the vast number of hours of spare time available to him and how he reviewed over and over every event of his then 28-year life that he could recall. In every case, he was able to think of ways he could have done better with just a tiny bit more effort. I think that is true of our customer service experiences as well. No matter how exceptional we are, there is always room for a 1 percent improvement.

The following exercise is designed to help you focus on small, incremental improvements to your service attitude and technique. You'll be surprised at how quickly these 1 percent improvements add up.

≈ The time needed to complete this exercise is 20 minutes.

Exercise

EXERCISE: THE 1 PERCENT SOLUTION

Instructions: Reflect back on your last five encounters with customers (in person or over the telephone). Think through how you handled each situation, then try and identify and write down something you could have done to improve your response by 1 percent.

Customer Situation	1% Improvement
1. Encountered a customer unhappy with the amount of his gas and electric bill.	I could have shown more empathy since everyone's bills are running high due to the extreme winter
2.	
3.	
4.	
5.	

LOOK FOR TRENDS

Another thing that Service Stars do is watch for trends. If four customers complain about something in a short period of time, there may be a problem or a process that needs to be fixed. Look for trends and report them to your coach, manager, or leader. Information, or data, is one of the most valuable tools available to an organization. In Chapter 11, we talked about feedback and how we should beg for it. Feedback is a form of data. The late W. Edwards Deming, whom we quoted elsewhere in this book, also had a favorite saying, "In God we trust, all others bring data." In business and industry, the entire basis of quality improvement is data-based decision making (rather than hunches and intuition). You can apply the same philosophy as you seek to constantly improve the quality of your service.

Here are a few examples of discovering trends:

★ An office assistant notices an increase in erroneous shipments from a particular office supply company and reports it to the purchasing department.

★ A nurse in the outpatient surgery department of a hospital notes an increase in telephone inquiries from patients about post-surgery wound care. Upon analyzing this data, the nurse discovers that the after-care information sheet sent home with patients is incomplete and needs to be revised.

★ A mechanic in the service department of a car dealership performs a large number of repairs to the transmission on a particular new car model. He reports the problem to management, which in turn notifies the manufacturer in time to make modifications on the assembly line.

In each of these cases, the frontline associate could easily have ignored the data and simply continued to deal with the problems (incorrect supplies, more patient phone calls, higher number of car repairs). The mark of a Service Star is that they notice the trend and tell someone about it.

TAKE INITIATIVE

While at a conference in Philadelphia recently, I stayed at a nice downtown hotel. Each morning, as I would walk through the lobby, I noticed that the bellman had a stack of towels and a supply of water bottles sitting on his counter. After a couple days, I asked him what the towels and water were for. He informed me that he has a lot of hotel guests who jog early in the morning, and they appreciate having a towel waiting for them upon their return, as well as a drink of water. Impressed with his creativity and innovation, I asked what made him start offering this service. He replied, "I thought to myself, what else can I do to make the early morning run more enjoyable for my customers?" No one told him to put towels and water out. He simply took the initiative because he knew it would make a positive impact on customer service. That's what Service Stars do.

BE CURIOUS

Another characteristic of associates creating customer value while advancing in their organizations is curiosity. Service Stars have an almost unstoppable sense of curiosity. They know their organization inside and out. They keep up-to-date on new products, new processes, and new policies. Rarely do they have to tell a customer, "I don't know, but I'll find out." They have made it their business to anticipate customer questions and find out the answers in advance. The more progressive, forward-thinking companies in this country ensure that associates are continually exposed to all aspects of the business, both during initial orientation and then periodically. Salespeople should work on the production line; inventory control clerks should take a turn in the warehouse; customer service representatives should spend some time on the shipping floor; managers should work everywhere. And if your organization doesn't have a program for this, seek out the opportunity. Think to yourself for a moment, "What department or branch in the organization do I know the least about or would I like to know more about?" "What can I do tomorrow to increase my knowledge and thereby my ability to add value for my customers?" Then just say, "I'm curious."

Notes

Note to managers and team leaders: Have you considered implementing a shadowing program for your associates? Do you encourage associates from other departments to visit your area? Who will you send and invite first?

Schedule a half or full day for an effective visit. After your associates return from a shadowing experience, ask what one or two things they learned that could improve your operation.

You and Your Team

In this section we want to provide some specific suggestions for things you can do at team meetings to build a stronger team and ensure that everyone is really working together to provide exceptional customer service.

Team Tips

★ Offer encouragement

★ Brainstorm solutions

★ Learn as a team

★ Discuss new policies and procedures

★ Identify areas for improvement

OFFER ENCOURAGEMENT

Customer care is a day-in, day-out profession. Sometimes it can be a grind. Stress and burnout are always a danger. Perhaps the most valuable thing you can do as team members is offer encouragement to one another, particularly during stressful periods. Let your coworkers know that you empathize with their feelings. Maybe one of them has just encountered a nasty customer and is ready to walk. Perhaps it's been a day of frustrating situations, constant lines, or telephone queues that wouldn't stop. Talk with each other, give encouragement, but by all means stay positive. Don't engage in gripe sessions. All that will do is drag down the entire team.

BRAINSTORM SOLUTIONS

From time to time you will encounter customer problems with no obvious solution, or challenging situations you haven't been confronted with before. Rather than spinning your wheels endlessly trying to find a solution, try bringing the problem or situation to a team meeting. Lay out the facts and ask for your team members' input. How would they handle the problem or situation? Someone may have been through the same situation recently and come up with a brilliant solution or phrase you can write down or post to use next time it comes up.

Team meetings should foster an environment in which it is OK to walk in and say, "Oh, I didn't do very well handling Mrs. Jones yesterday. Let me tell you how I messed up." Explain how you handled the situation and ask for input from team members on how you could have done better. This is a difficult thing to do because your ego is involved and it takes self-confidence to expose our shortcomings, especially to fellow team members. Experience is the best teacher, however, and you can learn and grow from your mistakes by letting others help. By the same token, don't be shy about parading a few successes out to the team. "Let me tell you what I did. It was so rewarding, and it worked! The customer loved it, and even sent me this letter saying so!" Again, there is a danger that you may come across as a braggart, but not if the environment has been set that encourages discussion of both failures and successes.

TEAM LEARNING

Another great idea is to set aside 10 to 15 minutes of every team meeting to learn something new. Maybe someone has a novel idea on how to handle a particular type of customer. Maybe someone has read an interesting article on some aspect of service that is worthy of sharing with the group. I recently stayed at the Marriott Hotel in New Orleans for a week and was impressed not only with the service but with the attitude and sense of teamwork of the staff. I asked several associates how they maintained that sense of unity and positive feeling towards customers. One of the first things they mentioned was the daily team meeting held early each morning. In addition to reviewing conventions and meetings currently in-house, as well as staffing assignments, the team takes time to discuss one of the Marriott "basics of the day." The day I inquired they were discussing "The Spirit to Serve," which they define as practicing teamwork and treating each other with the same respect they afford to their family and best customers. Their motto for the day was, "If we take care of each other, we will be able to take better care of our guests." Starting the day with some team training and discussion of core values can't help but put associates into the right customer care-oriented frame of mind.

DISCUSS NEW POLICIES AND PROCEDURES

Ho, hum! "Here's a new policy," says the team leader, "we need to discuss it this morning." How many times is that line recited each morning across corporate America? Here's a different twist, however. Instead of just listening to and trying to understand the new policy or procedure, discuss as a team how best to explain the new policy to the customer. If the billing cycle is being changed, for example, anticipate customer reactions, particularly objections they might have, and figure out together how best to make them understand. If prices or fees are going up on certain products or services, anticipate customers' reactions and how you will convince them that they are still getting great value for their money.

IDENTIFY AREAS FOR IMPROVEMENT

One of the best methods of coming up with areas for improvement is discussion at team meetings. You are the ones on the frontlines with the customers. You hear what they like, what they dislike, and what they think ought to be changed. In other words, take the verbal feedback you get from your customers on a daily basis and look at it critically. What changes could we make that might better serve the customer? Some of those changes might require management approval, while others can be implemented on the spot.

Remember, your customer service is only as strong as your team. Spending time together as a team, learning together, offering encouragement, and identifying areas for improvement, is time well spent because it gives us a chance to add value for our customers.

Remember: There Is No Silver Bullet

In this book we have talked about businesses from tire dealers to techno-logical forerunners. From the doctor's office to the major call center, each business has its own set of challenges in creating the total customer experience. What is an after-the-service red rose on the car seat to one is a creative note or Web site to another.

What is truly important in today's highly competitive world is to *do something*, no matter how large or small, to improve customer service. Make your Web site customer friendly; greet patrons with a warm, genuine smile; listen carefully to feedback; be patient with upset customers; make sure you answer your voice mails promptly. The list goes on and on. A few require an investment of dollars or the approval of management to implement. Most require only self-approval and an investment of your time and energy. Again, the key is to just do something. With so few doing much of anything to improve customer care, you'll be amazed at the difference you can make.

It's a Wrap

Did you catch all of the following points?

The Service Star: What does one look like?
★ Motivated to serve
★ Flexible
★ Energy and enthusiasm
★ Ownership

Great service is HABITual
★ Be consistent
★ Be creative
★ Love what you do
★ Pay attention to the details
★ Love change, chaos, and surprise
★ Recharge yourself

Moving up the customer service ladder
★ Be 1 percent better tomorrow than you are today
★ Watch for trends
★ Take the initiative
★ Be curious

Building a stronger service TEAM
★ Offer encouragement to each other
★ Brainstorm solutions to problems
★ Learn as a team
★ Discuss new policies and procedures
★ Identify improvement areas

Remember: There is no silver bullet.

Index